Business Schools Post-Covid-19

It all began when the world's first business school, the European School of Commerce Paris (ESCP), was established in 1819. Criticism notwithstanding, business schools have since continued their path in higher education without facing existential metamorphoses. Covid-19, however, has accelerated business schools' digital transformation, calling into question the concept of business school itself.

Business schools are in a new competitive landscape and profound structural changes seem inevitable. This concise text offers insights into how business schools should rethink their approach to management education, differentiate themselves from new players in the higher education market, and find innovative ways of doing things. The book is a survival toolkit for leadership teams across the world. It examines the rationale of business school and how it has evolved. The purpose of research is explained, and the teaching of management is explored. Kaplan analyzes the current business model in the digital environment. He looks at the business of accreditations and rankings and branding and community-building as strategies to address competition. The book concludes by looking at change leadership at business schools.

It will interest both leaders of established academic institutions and alternative educational providers from edtech and big tech planning to enter the management education market.

Andreas Kaplan is a globally recognized and widely published higher education expert with more than 15 years of leadership experience in academia. Currently President and Dean of Kühne Logistics University, Germany, Kaplan previously held the positions of Rector and Provost at ESCP Business School, Sorbonne Alliance.

Routledge Focus on Business and Management

The fields of business and management have grown exponentially as areas of research and education. This growth presents challenges for readers trying to keep up with the latest important insights. *Routledge Focus on Business and Management* presents small books on big topics and how they intersect with the world of business research.

Individually, each title in the series provides coverage of a key academic topic, whilst collectively, the series forms a comprehensive collection across the business disciplines.

Systems Thinking and Sustainable Healthcare Delivery
Ben Fong

Gender Diversity and Inclusion at Work
Divergent Views from Turkey
Zeynep Özsoy, Mustafa Şenyücel and Beyza Oba

Management and Visualisation
Seeing Beyond the Strategic
Gordon Fletcher

Knowledge Management and AI in Society 5.0
Manlio Del Giudice, Veronica Scuotto and Armando Papa

The Logistics Audit
Methods, Organization and Practice
Piotr Buła and Bartosz Niedzielski

Women's Social Entrepreneurship
Case Studies from the United Kingdom
Panagiotis Kyriakopoulos

Business Schools Post-Covid-19
A Blueprint for Survival
Andreas Kaplan

For more information about this series, please visit: www.routledge.com/ Routledge-Focus-on-Business-and-Management/book-series/FBM

Business Schools Post-Covid-19

A Blueprint for Survival

Andreas Kaplan

Routledge
Taylor & Francis Group

LONDON AND NEW YORK

First published 2024
by Routledge
4 Park Square, Milton Park, Abingdon, Oxon, OX14 4RN

and by Routledge
605 Third Avenue, New York, NY 10158

Routledge is an imprint of the Taylor & Francis Group, an informa business

British Library Cataloguing-in-Publication Data
A catalogue record for this book is available from the British Library

Library of Congress Cataloging-in-Publication Data
Names: Kaplan, Andreas, author.
Title: Business schools post-COVID-19 : a blueprint for survival / Andreas Kaplan.
Description: Abingdon, Oxon ; New York, NY : Routledge, 2023.
| Series: Routledge focus on business and management | Includes bibliographical references and index. |
Identifiers: LCCN 2023011847 (print) | LCCN 2023011848 (ebook) | ISBN 9781032381046 (hardback) | ISBN 9781032381053 (paperback) | ISBN 9781003343509 (ebook)
Subjects: LCSH: Business schools. | Business education. | Management--Study and teaching.
Classification: LCC HF1111 .K37 2023 (print) | LCC HF1111 (ebook) | DDC 650.071/1--dc23/eng/20230322
LC record available at https://lccn.loc.gov/2023011847
LC ebook record available at https://lccn.loc.gov/2023011848

ISBN: 9781032381046 (hbk)
ISBN: 9781032381053 (pbk)
ISBN: 9781003343509 (ebk)

DOI: 10.4324/9781003343509

Typeset in Times New Roman
by Deanta Global Publishing Services, Chennai, India

Contents

List of Abbreviations

AACSB	Association to Advance Collegiate Schools of Business
AI	Artificial Intelligence
AMBA	Association of MBAs
AoL	Assurance of Learning
BCG	Boston Consulting Group
BH	Business Horizons
BSc	Bachelor of Science
CEIBS	China-Europe International Business School
CEO	Chief Executive Officer
ChatGPT	Chat Generative Pre-training Transformer
CO₂	Carbon dioxide
Covid-19	Coronavirus Disease 2019
CRM	Customer Relationship Management
CSR	Corporate Social Responsibility
CV	Curriculum Vitae
DORA	Declaration On Research Assessment
EAP	École des Affaires de Paris
Edtech	Educational Technology
EFMD	European Foundation for Management Development
ENA	École Nationale d'Administration
EQUIS	EFMD Quality Improvement System
ESCP	European School of Commerce Paris
ESMOD	École Supérieure des arts et techniques de la Mode
ESSEC	École Supérieure des Sciences Économiques et Commerciales
FAQ	Frequently Asked Question
FT	*Financial Times*
G8	Group of Eight
GDP	Gross Domestic Product
HBR	*Harvard Business Review*
HEC	École des Hautes Études Commerciales
HR	Human Resources
IE University	Instituto de Empresa University
IIM	Indian Institute of Management

IMD	International Institute for Management Development
INSEAD	Institut Européen d'Administration des Affaires
INSP	Institut National du Service Public
IoT	Internet of Things
ITP	International Teachers Programme
KISS	Keep It Short and Simple
KLU	Kühne Logistics University
LBS	London Business School
LMS	Learning Management System
MBA	Master of Business Administration
MiM	Master in Management
MIT	Massachusetts Institute of Technology
MOOC	Massive Open Online Course
MPA	Master of Public Administration
MSc	Master of Science
PhD	Philosophiae Doctor
PLoS	Public Library of Science
PR	Public Relations
RRBM	Responsible Research in Business and Management
RSM	Rotterdam School of Management
SMOC	Synchronous Massive Online Course
SPOC	Small Private Online Course
SSOC	Synchronous Small Online Course
TEAL	Technology-Enabled Advanced Learning
UK	United Kingdom
US	United States
VR	Virtual Reality
WU Vienna	Wirtschaftsuniversität Vienna

List of Figures and Tables

Figures

Tables

Author Biography

Andreas Kaplan

Professor Andreas Kaplan is a higher education expert who has extensively published on the sector's general transformation as well as its digitalization, resting on more than 15 years of administration and leadership experience in academia.

Figure 0.1 Professor Andreas M. Kaplan

Currently, he serves as President and Dean of Kühne Logistics University (KLU) based in Hamburg, Germany. As former Rector and Provost of the European School of Commerce Paris (ESCP), the world's oldest business school, part of the Sorbonne Alliance, Kaplan was in charge of 6,000+ students across the School's six campuses in France, Germany, Italy, Poland, Spain, and the UK, and gained insights into a variety of higher education systems across Europe. His academic career began at the ESSEC Business School and Sciences Po Paris, with further teaching experience at Harvard, Humboldt, and Tsinghua Universities. Kaplan sits on the boards and strategic advisory committees of various higher education institutions and edtech start-ups nationally and internationally. He recurrently serves as advisor, consultant, and keynote speaker.

Kaplan's overall research addresses society's digital transformation, notably due to advances in artificial intelligence and social media communications. A high-profile PLoS study counts Kaplan within the group of most cited and impactful scientists in the world. According to John Wiley & Sons, Kaplan figures among the top 50 management and business authors globally. His seminal work coining and defining the term "social media" has repeatedly been the most downloaded publication of the roughly 15 million scientific articles in the world's largest research database, Elsevier's Science Direct, spanning a multitude of disciplines including data science, engineering, management, medicine, and psychology. Kaplan's work has been published by Cambridge, Harvard, and Oxford University Press.

A European at heart, Andreas M. Kaplan has worked and resided in Austria, France, Germany, Italy, Portugal, Spain, the UK, and the US. Kaplan did his Habilitation at the Panthéon-Sorbonne University and his PhD at the University of Cologne and HEC Paris. Holder of an MPA (Master of Public Administration) from the École Nationale d'Administration (ENA, Institut National du Service Public – INSP), an MBA from ThePower Business School (ThePower MBA), an MSc from ESCP, and a BSc from the Ludwig-Maximilians-University Munich, Kaplan additionally did part of his doctoral studies at INSEAD and graduated from the ITP at Northwestern University's Kellogg School of Management. He served on the board of the German-French Economic Circle and is a founding member of the European Center for Digital Competitiveness.

Foreword: Business Schools' Survival Blueprint

It all began when the world's first business school, the European School of Commerce Paris (ESCP), today part of the Sorbonne Alliance, was founded in 1819, more than 200 years ago. University of Pennsylvania's Wharton School of Management and HEC Paris followed in 1881. Contrary to what one might have thought, likely the globally best-known business school, Harvard, was not established until 1908. Today there are more than 13,000 business schools worldwide, and much has changed since their inception. ESCP, for example, now into its third century of existence, transformed over time from an originally French-based management school into a multi-country, multi-campus institution with campuses in Berlin, London, Madrid, Paris, Turin, and Warsaw.

From their founding onwards, business schools have endured critique and fight for their legitimacy. At their establishment, many doubted that management could be taught from a theoretical and conceptual perspective in a classroom instead of on the job and by a learning-by-doing approach. On the opposite end of the theory > practice continuum, scholars from more established disciplines questioned the academic quality of the as-yet unrecognized field of management science. Even today, much criticism surrounds the relatively limited relevance of business schools' research output, as well as the applicability of course content to the business world, often described as distant from corporate needs and future job market requirements. Further examples of negative judgment concern business schools having difficulty leaving behind them a reputation for educating mainly profit-aiming managers who lack critical thinking capacities, not to mention humanity.

Yet both justified and unjustified criticism notwithstanding, business schools continue to exist owing to continuous and successful adaptation. In response to charges of not being "academic enough," for example, the initially practice-oriented business schools entered research and knowledge production, especially since the 1950s/1960s. When blamed in part for the 2008 financial crisis, allegedly having produced ruthless and unethical graduates, business schools responded by strengthening their teaching of business ethics and corporate social responsibility (CSR). More recently, they began integrating sustainability into their curricula in response to the trend of youth seeking and aspiring to a more eco-responsible lifestyle, economy, and society.

Via these continuous revisions and alterations, business schools have continued their path in the higher education landscape, without facing existential metamorphoses and fundamental mutation…up until now. However, the sector's rapid digitalization, strongly accelerated and propelled by the Covid-19 pandemic, might be a game-changer, necessitating more profound modification to counter potential disruption and likely turmoil in sight. While there are regional differences in how the pandemic affected higher education, in all cases, it threw its digitalization into high gear. One could even claim that the advent of the pandemic in 2019, exactly 200 years after the inception of the business school, is not merely a coincidence, but a symbolic call for its resolute reinvention.

Not only did the pandemic alter the mindsets of learners regarding online courses to which they previously were strongly disinclined, but it also increased competition and brought new players from edtech and big tech to the fore. Compelled to stay at home during lockdowns, people sought to use their consequent free time to learn and acquire new skills and competencies. However, instead of turning to business schools, learners mostly tried alternatives such as LinkedIn Learning, Coursera, Google's Career Certificates, or start-ups such as ThePowerMBA, due to their appealing, shorter, and significantly less costly online courses and programs. During the same period, business schools saw their continuing education demands decrease, some more, some less depending upon locale.

Consequently, like many entities, business schools are facing and increasingly will face a new, competitive landscape in the pandemic's aftermath. Profound structural changes seem inevitable to cope with these trends and developments for management schools to stay relevant in the long term. Business schools need to ensure that their graduates exhibit stronger skills, competence, and know-how than one could obtain by completing certificates issued by edtech and big tech players. Only if this is the case will business schools be able to justify their far higher tuition fees and significantly longer program durations. One might say that this was already the case pre-Covid. Yet, business school critics frequently question the usefulness and (positive) impact of their succeeding in graduating well-performing future managers and leaders.

Business schools will accordingly need to rethink their approach to management education and science, differentiate themselves from those new players rapidly entering the higher education market, and find a new rationale, or *raison d'être*, as well as new ways of doing things. Historically, when ESCP invented the business school concept, there was a reason for its creation: universities did not want and were not able to respond to the increasing need for a new kind of professional, i.e., the manager. Over time, the focus on teaching and student-centricity gave way to research, partly pushed by the desire to obtain accreditations and be highly ranked in both national and international league tables. Business schools' entire context has therefore changed. It's time for its reinvention, the moment to define its new future purpose and role within the economy and society. Business schools must respond to the oft-heard allegation that they are redundant. They need to create value-added student experiences and serve as educators of well-rounded, well-trained, ethical, and responsible managers able to lead in an environment characterized by climate change, migration, automation and advances in artificial intelligence, to mention just a view of today's global challenges.

Based on my research on management education, my leadership experience as Dean, Rector, and Professor, but also as a student at various business schools, as well as a board member of higher education institutions and edtech companies, I seek to provide insight into the business of business schools, providing an overview of what a business school currently is and what, in my opinion, it ought to become. I will do so from two perspectives: the one of business school practice, and the other of higher education science. Unsurprisingly, I am influenced by the environment wherein I have studied and worked for more than two decades. Accordingly, this work should be read keeping in mind that its author is a European business school and university president, research-active and international in his outlook. Nonetheless, I belief that this book provides many insights and food for thought for both business schools with similar contexts, as well as those that differ from my experience. Think of this book as a business school survival superkit: a guide to not only survive but thrive in this new era characterized by the sector's deep (digital) transformation.

Comprising nine chapters, all intended as ideas and inspiration for those involved in the area of business schools and management education, this book sets forth a business school's rationale and *raison d'être*, and how change has occurred over time (Chapter 1). Its current business model is analyzed (Chapter 2), and the new digital environment is decrypted (Chapter 3). The aim and purpose of management research will be explained (Chapter 4), the teaching of business and management examined (Chapter 5), and the functioning and business of accreditations and rankings evaluated (Chapter 6). Branding (Chapter 7) and Bonding (Chapter 8) will be presented as barriers to incoming competitors. Finally, business school administration and leadership will be explored (Chapter 9). Note that this book's chapters are available as stand-alone texts, which leads to some – but kept to a minimum – redundancy, so as to facilitate their stand-alone comprehension.

It has been an immense pleasure to write this book and put down my thoughts and experiences on paper. I want to thank everybody who participated in my professional journey in the business school environment and

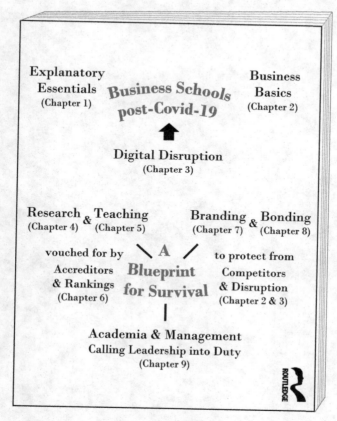

Figure 0.2 Foreword: Business Schools Post-Covid-19

shaped my ideas through discussions, debates, joint projects, and simply working together. Readers might disagree with my conclusions, dislike my argumentation, or believe my analyses to be exaggerated or sensationalist. Indeed, I might be partly, or even entirely, wrong; none of us can foretell the future, and only time will tell. Nonetheless, I hope that this book will provide you with what I intend: vision, intellectual nourishment, perspective and outlook, encouragement, and (why not?) optimism and hope.

1 The Business School's Rationale and *Raison d'Être*

To a certain degree, the statement could be made that management institutions have not substantially changed since the European School of Commerce Paris (ESCP) – the world's first and still-operating business school – was established in 1819 (Blanchard 2009; Passant 2018, 2019). Over the past two centuries, business schools' features have remained relatively untouched, although some discussion exists as to what those precisely are. Put simply, a business school is a higher education institution that offers degrees in business management and administration. Business schools are also called management schools, or more colloquially, biz schools or b-schools. Some are stand-alone; others are affiliated with universities. Among the world's best-known business schools are Columbia Business School, Harvard Business School, Kellogg School of Management at Northwestern University, MIT's Sloan School of Management, Stanford Graduate School of Business, and University of Pennsylvania's Wharton School.

Business schools traditionally teach accounting, finance, human resources, marketing, strategy, and supply chain management, to mention just a few. Many produce knowledge via their faculty's scientific research and publications. While English-speaking business schools offer the MBA – or Master of Business Administration – as their flagship degree, European institutions are more likely to offer a Master in Management. Regardless, most business schools now offer an entire array, from general to more specialized management degrees, from undergraduate and graduate to doctoral studies and executive education certificates. Business schools have been derisively described as "manager mills" that groom a preselected group of students (the input), into certified graduates as output (Hawawini 2005). I prefer to think of them as a building with four corners, and the future inside (Kaplan 2018a).

To understand the business schools' rationale and *raison d'être*, and to comprehend what they are currently facing with the Covid-19 pandemic having prompted increased competition with entrants from the ed and big tech sector at the fore (Kaplan 2021 a, b), a look at business schools' past is a good starting point (Kaplan 2014). To do so, we refer to four periods, based on the historical evolution of management schools' teaching-research paradigm. It is argued that history, to some extent, is repeating itself with the pandemic

DOI: 10.4324/9781003343509-1

having triggered a new stage in business schools' annals. Although generally speaking, one can claim that management schools are rather generic, or put otherwise, "different, but same-same," four points illustrating business schools' various forms are applied to establish a classification scheme for business schools (Kaplan 2018a). Such categorization facilitates the correct application of the presented recommendations and advice regarding how business schools can survive and thrive in the digital era. Finally, four figures in a business school's ecosystem are identified, their motivations analyzed, and their relative dominance and weight illustrated. A sound understanding of stakeholders' interests and importance further helps assess the specific context wherein management schools are henceforth operating.

1.1   History Repeating

While with the Industrial Revolution businesses grew, ownerships changed, and a need for trained managers evolved (Khurana and Khanna 2005; McNamara 2014), universities could not and did not want to educate students for this new profession. Consequently a new educational institution – a school teaching business – was needed (de Fournas 2007; Renouard 1920). Contrary to what you might assume, the birthplace of the business school was not the US, but rather France, on December 1, 1819, when the European School of Commerce Paris (ESCP) opened its doors (Blanchard 2009). While there were earlier attempts to establish institutions in management education, they stopped or shut down after a couple of years. Therefore, ESCP invented the (successful) business school concept and began its first historical period, characterized by a strong focus on vocational training. Its curriculum initially included accounting, arithmetic, foreign languages, geography, and writing skills: all competencies needed for commercial activities. The pedagogical approach was highly practical, with lots of exercises and simulation games, possibly prefiguring the case study, which is still used today in business schools. The business school's rationale was pedagogy, and the students were taught toward entering skilled commercial, entrepreneurial, and managerial roles.

   The US business schools especially, with their pioneer, the Wharton School, established in 1881, were strongly criticized for this very practical approach to learning and teaching management. In contrast to mostly standalone European business schools, their US counterparts were collegiate, i.e., part of a university, and therefore strongly accused by faculties of established disciplines of lowering the respective universities' academic standards (Engwall and Zamagni 1998). Thus, Harvard Business School's establishment in 1908 was met with considerable resistance, with many scholars citing the inappropriateness of its affiliation with a university committed to the sciences and liberal arts. One Harvard University alumnus even voiced his critical assessment in lyrical form, ridiculing this decision as:

Fair Harvard! I hear that you have been such a fool
As to start a ridiculous Business School.

In response, US schools sought to become more scientific and academic in their orientation, laying the cornerstone for business schools' second era: the period of wisdom. The 1959 Gordon-Howell report, blaming American business schools' low academic standards and their lack of analytical and managerial emphasis, finally prompted and accelerated this quest for scientific reputation and recognition, not only in the US, but later on worldwide (Kaplan 2014, 2015). Research gradually became the business school's focus, subsequently reducing its focus on students. Faculty research sidelined pedagogical quality and the transmission of directly applicable professional skills and competencies.

To a certain degree, international accreditation bodies such as the AACSB, EFMD (EQUIS), and AMBA, and especially rankings, strengthened this trend of the scientization of business schools (Bennis and O'Toole 2005; Kaplan 2015). While the accreditation bodies aimed to ensure the pedagogical quality of programs and courses, and improve transparency among the broad offerings of business schools, the actual effect was somewhat mitigated (Wedlin 2007). In international rankings such as those issued by the *Financial Times* (the FT ranking), *Business Week*, the *Wall Street Journal*, and *The Economist*, teaching quality holds hardly any weight. The reason therefore is simple: teaching impact is inherently difficult to measure, whereas other indicators, such as research output, are much more quantifiable and objective. Even students themselves, when asked whether they were satisfied with their experience at a given business school, in most cases respond positively, knowing that responding otherwise could cause their alma mater to drop in the rankings, which would consequently have a negative effect on the respondent. Nonetheless, accreditations and rankings have many positive effects (Gibbons, Neumayer, and Perkins 2015; Gregoir 2011), as exemplified by the 2008 financial crisis, another landmark in business school history that led to contemplation and self-examination (Cornuel and Hommel 2012). Blamed for being partly responsible for training unethical managers, many courses on ethics and corporate social responsibility have since been incorporated into syllabi and curricula (O'Connor 2013), doubtlessly also prompted by accreditation bodies and rankings gradually including such criteria in their evaluation grids. This stage in the evolution of business schools can be called the period of vouching, business schools' quality being vouched for – or not – by both accreditors and rankings.

The next era in the history of management education, called the (partly) virtual period, was induced by the Covid-19 pandemic, which significantly threw into high gear the sector's digital transformation (Cornuel 2022; Kaplan 2022 a,b). While MOOCs, SPOCs, and other online courses have been around for some time (Kaplan and Haenlein 2016; Kaplan 2017), many institutions

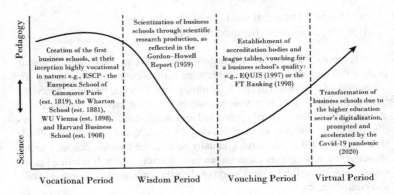

Figure 1.1 Business School History: Four Periods

were reluctant to broadly enter the digital sphere pre-pandemic. Then the pandemic hit, compelling professors and students to stay home and in front of their computer screens. During this involuntary seclusion, many faculty members and students learned about the virtual world's positive aspects. Now there's no turning back the clock: online courses and the higher education digital environment are here to stay. This new reality and context might restore the focus to pedagogy, thereby recalibrating the importance of faculty's teaching and research activities. In brief, the digitalization of courses renders them far more visible and testable. While previously, one's pedagogical skills – or lack thereof – stayed largely behind closed classroom doors, now they are viewable on Coursera, YouTube, and even TikTok (Kaplan 2020). Thus 2020, the year of business schools entering their third century, might re-shift business schools' focus toward their students, i.e., we circled back to our inception, or put differently: history repeated itself (Khurana 2007; Nohria and Khurana 2008).

1.2   Different, But Same-Same

When describing the business school's rationale, note that there is no one type of management school, so specific analyses and recommendations possibly do not apply to all of them, as business schools take a variety of forms: some are standalone; some are collegiate. Some are private; others are public institutions. Some – but not all – produce scientific knowledge. Some provide continuing education; others do not. These are just some of the various differences found in the business school landscape, so specificities must be taken into account when decrypting their future evolution in this digital era. While my orientation comes from an international, multi-country, research-active business school, this book's perspective is admittedly biased, nonetheless its analyses aim at providing food for thought and perspective for all kinds of management schools. To illustrate business schools' differing forms, four pointers are applied, facilitating the mapping of business schools along four dimensions, which I call the "Four Corners," and which refer to the aforementioned description of management institutions as buildings with four corners and the future inside: Content, Capital, Culture, and Compass (Kaplan 2018).

"Content" indicates where on the teaching > research continuum a school is located. While it is impossible to call oneself a school without teaching something, there are institutions that are not engaged in research. In most cases, such schools have relatively higher enrollment and larger class sizes. Research, in contrast, is time-intensive and costly, thus potentially decreasing the bottom line and necessitating extensive funding, some of which comes from tuition. The top-tier schools especially pour significant resources into research. Some research-intensive institutions choose to overemphasize the importance of publications and consequently neglect pedagogy and their students (Bennis and O'Toole 2005). Pure teaching schools, on the other hand, being student-centric in nature, might have a strong hand in facing the sector's disruptive movements. But research-active schools have another advantage: research production enables them to strongly differentiate themselves from non-academic/alternative providers from the ed- and big-tech sectors, transforming and potentially disrupting the management education sector. In any case, as in all disciplines, finding the optimal equilibrium between research and teaching is a recurring discussion among business school deans, administration, and faculty.

"Capital" refers to a given institution's financial resources (d'Alessio and Avolio 2011). Business schools can be either publicly or privately funded through tuition, endowments, and/or the state (Iñiguez de Onzoño 2011). While standalone institutions mostly disburse and have total control over their various income sources, for collegiate business schools, it is not uncommon to transfer some of their revenues to other, less equipped faculties within the respective university. Moreover, it would not be surprising that traditional business metrics such as the analysis of margins are more present in the business school environment than they are in other disciplines, thereby occupying a chunk of business school administrators' time. Naturally, management schools that benefit from a higher share of secured public funding, i.e., that are less dependent on tuition and student recruitment, are less vulnerable to potentially disruptive movements in the sector and in the economy generally.

Concerning "Culture," business schools can be defined as either pursuing the US or the European model, i.e., the two world regions wherein their origins lie. As aforementioned, most US business schools are collegiate in nature, while European schools are often standalone institutions, although exceptions exist. Differences furthermore are characterized by the singular economic, political, and social context prevailing in the US versus Europe. Generally, it can be said that European schools focus more on cross-cultural considerations, societal aspects, and an interdisciplinary approach to teaching and learning than do those following the US model (Kaplan 2014, 2018b). A more wholistic view of management education might prove advantageous in business schools' future (Pudelko and Harzing 2007) as, for instance, job markets require increasing adaptability and flexibility and employees being capable of autodidacticism and adjusting rapidly to new contexts and situations. Culture in this sense is unrelated to an institution's geographic location, i.e., schools in Europe can apply the US model and vice versa. Culture also applies to institutions based elsewhere, considering some local adjustments, with Asia especially containing an increasing number of highly ranked business schools, two examples being the Indian Institutes of Management (IIMs) or CEIBS and Tsinghua University in China (Schlegelmilch 2020).

"Compass" denotes an institution's international richness (e.g., cultural diversity in faculty or student body) and reach (e.g., percentage of international students and students studying abroad), and is used for categorization purposes (Hawawini 2005). Business schools are located somewhere on a continuum, with local schools at one end and global schools at the other. While local and regional institutions are characterized by relatively low international richness and reach, at global and highly international business schools, one can find faculty and students from all over the world. Both types have their strong points against the backdrop of an increasingly digitalized and competitive environment. International/global schools likely benefit from higher brand equity, rendering them better able to attract students worldwide into their offline and, even more so, online programs. They also might be more affected, positively or negatively, by the sector's digital transformation as a result of so-called techno-globalism (Ostry and Nelson 1995), i.e., the development of common behavioral patterns and values in people from differing backgrounds through exposure to social media in particular and the internet in general (Friedman 2005, Rugman and Oh 2008). In contrast, regional and local schools might be less threatened by business schools' digital transformation, since they are more adapted to the opposing trend of de-globalization (Petricevic and Teece 2019).

However, while differences among business schools certainly exist, from an outside, lay perspective, one could claim that they all are much alike. Even as a business school expert, it is not straightforward to immediately cite salient differences between such schools as Oxford's Saïd Business School or Cambridge's Judge Business School; the Wharton School or Kellogg School of Management; HEC Paris or IE Business School; WU Vienna or the University of St. Gallen: they all teach business, providing the same kinds of (core) courses in Finance, Marketing, Supply Chain Management, and Strategy; they all educate future managers and business leaders; and they all cultivate large networks of alumni and long-standing partnerships with companies. While this "different, but same-same" philosophy might have worked in the past, continuing that approach could be risky in the post-pandemic era,

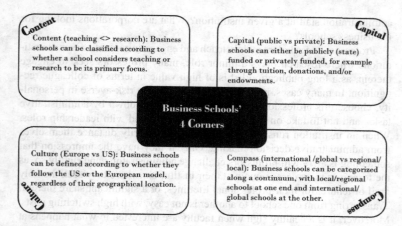

Figure 1.2 Business School Classification: Four Pointers and "Corners"

when all business schools are challenged by the sector's digital transformation and an increasingly fierce competitive landscape.

Certainly the pandemic did not have the same impact on all higher education institutions worldwide. Due to differences in government regulations, in some countries (e.g., Spain), universities were only marginally locked down compared to others, which almost permanently shifted to online teaching (e.g., Germany). Some countries (e.g., Estonia) were much more prepared for the virtual environment than others as a result of their general societies' more advanced digital transformation pre-pandemic. These examples only represent differences within Europe; we might expect discrepancies across world regions to be even stronger. Yet, the claim is made that digitalization and increased competition from alternative educational providers, mostly online, might have a potentially disruptive impact on the entire management school landscape; and this sooner rather than later.

1.3   Stakeholder (A)symmetry

An organization achieves high legitimacy when all stakeholders' needs and expectations are satisfied. Accordingly, to understand the business school's rationale, we need to understand its main stakeholders. Four stakeholder groups will be examined in detail: scholars, students (including alumni), staff, and society at large, including partner organizations, government actors, and the broader public. These are all components of a business school's ecosystem, and their respective desires and motivations need to be balanced and coordinated. What are professors expecting from their institution? Why do students, i.e., future alumni, enroll in a given business school? What characterizes administration staff at a given institution? What are corporations looking for in business schools?

Professors and scholars mainly teach and engage in research. Even at institutions where research plays a minor role, many professors seek to engage therein, as a long publication list is of high value in terms of colleague recognition. In many cases, professors, often somewhat risk-averse in personality, choose this profession so as not to be weighed down by administrative tasks, and not to take on the responsibility associated with leadership roles. When an institution runs smoothly, faculty voluntarily distance themselves from administrative decision-making. Only if they have the impression that something is awry will professors challenge administrators; and rightly so, as the former in most cases remain at their institution, where they seek the holy grail of tenure, for their professional lifetimes, or a significant share thereof. Transferring from one school to another is not easy, with high switching costs. Moreover, it is a healthy sign when faculty are interested in what happens at their institution; the opposite would be detrimental.

When asking why students enroll in a given business school, we want the response to be "to learn management and business." The reality is, however, somewhat otherwise. Having asked this question to several students, the answers always surround experiencing student life and building a network, getting a degree from a reputable institution, and/or finding their dream job. In most cases, unfortunately, receiving a good education is rarely mentioned. This should perk up our antennae. Note that executive education participants have slightly different expectations and motivations to enroll in business school: they indeed want to acquire new, preferably recipe-like knowledge, skills, and competencies (much more than undergraduates); and like undergraduates, they seek the networking, participate in team-building exercises, and wish to engage in some fun activities. Both students and alumni are alike in their desire to obtain and continue receiving good internship and job offers due to having a certain institution's name on their CVs. Therefore, they want their institution to stay well-ranked and maintain a good reputation.

Non-academic staff obviously seek a pleasant work environment that is both motivating and stimulating. Some work in support functions such as accounting, human resources, or logistics. Others market and brand an institution or program, work in student recruiting and admissions, or maintain the physical plant. Often, however, they feel unvalued and have the impression that they come third and last in the importance of internal stakeholders after faculty and students. This is demotivating and leads to higher turnover and low employee retention rates, comparable to a corporate setting. While for many professors and by definition for students and future alumni, the business school is their alma mater for life, in the careers of administrative staff, it often represents only one stage of their working life.

Finally, business schools – especially since the 2008 financial crisis – are expected to play a pronounced role in society, holding strong stances on global warming, migration, inclusion, and diversity. In that regard, business schools' relationship with the broader public is increasingly under scrutiny, and must be addressed (Cornuel 2022). Companies and other organizations want to recruit students able to do the jobs for which they are hired; and to facilitate their recruiting efforts, they require and expect some preselection by the academic institution's admissions, and seek out graduates of a given business school who exhibit a solid set of skills and competencies. They recruit students from a given business school for a reason, and expect a specific profile consistent with their HR requirements. While organizations might also be interested in research collaborations or co-branding activities, their focus is nonetheless on sourcing talent. Last but not least, government and public administration expect business schools to adhere to legal and regulatory requirements in place for higher education institutions, ensuring academic quality on the one hand, and possibly constraining and inhibitive to (pedagogical) innovation on the other (Pucciarelli and Kaplan 2016, 2017, 2019).

Among these various players, professors are often viewed as the most salient group of stakeholders for at least three reasons: firstly, as aforementioned, they frequently remain at their institution for a lifetime, while students graduate and grow more distant from their alma mater's issues. Alumni are in many cases connected to their alma mater only via its appearance on their CV. Administrative staff often also quit seeking opportunities elsewhere. In brief, professors simply stay the longest at their institutions. Secondly, at least at research-intensive business schools, professors' publications help obtain funding and secure reputation and esteem, while pedagogy and student-centricity are harder to quantify. Thirdly, a business school's top leadership team

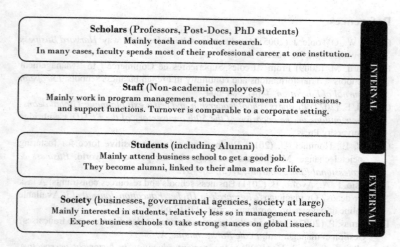

Figure 1.3 Business School Stakeholders: Four Principal Participants

is in most cases comprised of faculty members and academics, consciously or unconsciously favoring their former and likely future colleagues, as often academics in leadership roles resume their duties as professors after a couple of years of serving in administrative roles.

Increasingly, a more nuanced picture among these various groups (re) appears, shifting influence from scholars to the other three stakeholders, i.e., moving from stakeholder asymmetry to increased stakeholder symmetry (Kaplan 2021a). Firstly, many institutions are evolving toward student-centricity due to students confronted with ever-climbing tuition fees, with entry-level salaries not keeping pace. Consequently, students become more demanding. Also, due to the sector's fiercely competitive landscape, attracting students becomes tougher, thus giving them more weight. Institutions also have become aware of the importance of alumni and their demands for continuing education (Kaplan 2021b) as well as the associated revenue potential, incentivizing them to treat their graduates more cautiously. Alumni, moreover, are becoming universities' brand ambassadors, thereby reducing the need for high and increasingly scarce marketing budgets, as well as act as donors. Alumni also help in providing students with internships and their first jobs. With some companies having begun to do their sourcing in-house (cf., Google's Career Certificates), strong links to alumni are ever more crucial. Last but certainly not least, administrative staff becomes more important as well. With competition increasing and funding declining, expertise and experience in various support functions have become essential. Regarding this, Scott Galloway boldly pointed out, "The most value-added part of a university is not the professors; it's the admissions department" (Walsh 2020).

References

Bennis, W., O'Toole, J. (2005) How business schools lost their way. *Harvard Business Review, 83*(5), 96–104.

Blanchard, M. (2009) From "Ecoles Supérieures de Commerce" to "Management Schools": Transformations and continuity in French business schools. *European Journal of Education, 44*(4), 586–604.

Cornuel, E. (2022) *Business school leadership and crisis exit planning: Global deans' contributions on the occasion of the 50th anniversary of the EFMD.* Cambridge University Press.

Cornuel, E., Hommel, U. (2012) Business schools as a positive force for fostering societal change: Meeting the challenges of the post-crisis world. *Business & Professional Ethics Journal, 31*(2), 289–312.

D'Alessio, F. A., Avolio, B. (2011) Business schools and resources constraints: A task for deans? Or magicians? *Research in Higher Education Journal, 13,* Available online at www.aabri.com/manuscripts/11912.pdf.

De Fournas, P. (2007) Quelle identité pour les grandes écoles de commerce françaises? Gestion et management. *École Polytechnique, X.*

Engwall, L., Zamagni, V. (1998). *Management education in historical perspective.* Manchester University Press.

Friedman, T. L. (2005) *The world is flat: A brief history of the twenty-first century*. Farrar, Straus, and Giroux.

Gibbons, S., Neumayer, E., Perkins, R. (2015) Student satisfaction, league tables, and university applications: Evidence from Britain. *Economics of Education Review, 48*, 148–164.

Gordon R. A., Howell J. E. (1959) *Higher education for business*. Columbia University Press.

Gregoir S. (2011) *Business school rankings and business relevance: An overlooked dimension*. EDHEC Business School.

Hawawini G. (2005) The future of business schools. *Journal of Management Development, 24*(9), 770–782.

Iñiguez de Onzoño, S. (2011) *The learning curve: How business schools are re-inventing education*. Palgrave Macmillan.

Kaplan, A. (2014) European management and European business schools: Insights from the history of business schools. *European Management Journal, 32*(4), 529–534.

Kaplan, A. (2015) *European business and management (Vol. IV): Business education and scholarly research*. Sage Publications, Ltd.

Kaplan, A. (2017) Academia goes social media - MOOC, SPOC, SMOC, and SSOC: The digital transformation of higher education institutions and universities. In B. Rishi, S. Bandyopadhyay (eds.), *Contemporary issues in social media marketing*. Routledge.

Kaplan, A. (2018a) "A school is a building that has 4 walls – with tomorrow inside": Toward the reinvention of the business school. *Business Horizons, 61*(4), 599–608.

Kaplan, A. (2018b) Toward a theory of European business culture: The case of management education at the ESCP Europe Business School. In S. Gabriele, R. Monica, L. Johan (eds.), *The Routledge companion to European business* (pp. 113–124). Routledge.

Kaplan, A. (2020) Your attention, please: You've got 15 seconds! TikTok and how organizations can make use of it. In S. Kolukirik (ed.), *Digitalization and future of digital society* (pp. 367–378). Peter Lang Publishing House.

Kaplan, A. (2021a) Higher education at the crossroads of disruption: The university of the 21st century. In *Great debates in higher education*. Emerald Publishing.

Kaplan, A. (2021b) *Professionals need to keep their skills fresh. Will they turn to higher ed?* Harvard Business Publishing, September 17, 2021, available online at https://www.hbsp.harvard.edu/inspiring-minds/professionals-need-to-keep-their-skills-fresh-will-they-turn-to-higher-ed/?ab=top_nav.

Kaplan, A. (2022a) *Artificial intelligence, business, and civilization: Our fate made in machines*. Routledge.

Kaplan, A. (2022b) *Digital transformation and disruption of higher education*. Cambridge University Press.

Kaplan, A., Haenlein, M. (2016) Higher education and the digital revolution: MOOCs, SPOCs, social media, and the Cookie Monster. *Business Horizons, 59*(4), 441–450.

Khurana, R. (2007) *From higher aims to hired hands: The social transformation of American business schools and the unfulfilled promise of management as a profession* (p. 29). Princeton University Press.

Khurana, R., Khanna, T. (2005) *Harvard Business School and the making of a new profession*. Harvard Business School Publishing.

McNamara, P. (2014) Why business schools exist: On the intellectual origins of business schools in nineteenth-century France and America. In L. Trepanier (ed.), *The free market and the human condition: Essays on economics and culture* (pp. 103–120). Lexington Books.

Nohria N., Khurana R. (2008) It's time to make management a true profession. *Harvard Business Review, 86*, 70–77.

O'Connor S. (2013) The responsibility of business schools in training ethical leaders. *Forbes,* May 15.

Ostry, S., Nelson, R. R. (1995) *Techno-nationalism and techno-globalism: Conflict and cooperation, integrating national economies: Promise and pitfalls.* Brookings Institution Press.

Passant, A. (2018) Between filial piety and managerial opportunism: The strategic use of the history of a family business after the buyout by non-family purchasers. *Entreprises et Histoire, 91*(2), 62–81.

Passant, A. (2019) The early emergence of European commercial education in the nineteenth century: Insights from higher engineering schools. *Business History, 61*(7), 1–32.

Petricevic, O., Teece, D. J. (2019) The structural reshaping of globalization: Implications for strategic sectors, profiting from innovation, and the multinational enterprise. *Journal of International Business Studies, 50*, 1487–1512.

Pucciarelli, F., Kaplan, A. (2016) Competition and strategy in higher education: Managing complexity and uncertainty. *Business Horizons, 59*(3), 311–320.

Pucciarelli, F., Kaplan, A. (2017) Le Università Europee oggi: Sfide e nuove strategie, *Economia & Management*, gennaio/febbraio, *1*, 85–95.

Pucciarelli, F., Kaplan, A. (2019) Competition in higher education. In B. Nguyen, T. C. Melewar, J. Hemsley-Brown (eds.), *Strategic brand management in higher education.* Routledge.

Pudelko, M., Harzing, A.-W. (2007) How European is management in Europe? An analysis of past, present, and future management practices in Europe. *European Journal of International Management, 1*(3), 206–224.

Renouard, A. (1920) *Histoire de l'École Supérieure de Commerce de Paris (1820–1898)* (vol. *1899*, 2ème éd.) Au Siège de l'Association des Anciens Élèves.

Rugman, A., Oh, C. H. (2008) Friedman's follies: Insights on the globalization/regionalization debate. *Business and Politics, 10*(2), 1–14.

Schlegelmilch, B. (2020) Why business schools need radical innovations: Drivers and development trajectories. *Journal of Marketing Education, 42*(2), 93–107.

Walsh, J. D. (2020) The coming disruption: Scott Galloway predicts a handful of elite cyborg universities will soon monopolize higher education. *Intelligencer,* May 11.

Wedlin, L. (2007). The role of rankings in codifying a business school template: Classifications, diffusion, and mediated isomorphism in organizational fields. *European Management Review, 4*, 24–39.

2 Seemingly At Stake

The Business Of Business Schools

Today, most business schools face several challenges. For one, business schools are still criticized for not providing students with adequate training for becoming responsible, ethical leaders, and for not instructing them enough to integrate sustainability into their managerial choices. Although much has been done since the 2008 financial crisis, there is still room for improvement (Pucciarelli and Kaplan 2022). Generally speaking, business schools do not teach what they should teach (e.g., Datar, Garvin, and Cullen 2010; Ghoshal 2005; Khurana and Spender 2012; Locke and Spender 2011; Mintzberg 2004; Parker 2018; Simons 2013). Research at business schools is also not viewed very positively, and is still in many cases considered limited in its managerial and societal impact (Bennis and O'Toole 2005; Eckhardt and Wetherbe 2014; Glick, Tsui, and Davis 2018; Jack 2020; Shapiro and Kirkman 2018; Wilson and Thomas 2012). While the recent establishment of the Responsible Research in Business and Management (RRBM) network, devoted to encouraging, inspiring, and supporting useful and relevant business and managerial research, has brought this long-existing issue back onto the table, there is certainly much work ahead for business schools to produce more impactful and relevant research (RRBM Network 2022). Finally, tuition is rising due to reduced (public) funding (especially in Europe) and an increased need for budgets, with notably accreditation bodies and rankings increasingly demanding value for money paid in their requirements and performance indicators. Such developments gather a lot of negative voices, all the more as tuition at most institutions has increased far more rapidly than have their graduates' starting salaries (Kaplan 2014, 2018). In response, business schools try to rectify this by balancing high tuition fees with financial aid.

While all of these challenges are constantly on business school deans' minds, none have been fundamentally disruptive in magnitude. The sector's digital transformation, in contrast, might well be (Kaplan 2022). With the emergence of online courses and the application of artificial intelligence (AI) to higher education, the idea of knowledge transmission is called into question (Kaplan and Haenlein 2016; Kaplan 2017). While for centuries, teaching consisted mainly of an instructor and his or her students being in the same classroom at the same moment, the online world overcomes these limitations

DOI: 10.4324/9781003343509-2

of time and space. As recently as 2012, *The New York Times* proclaimed the year of the MOOC (Pappano 2012). Alongside, experts forecasted dooming digital days for business schools and for universities in general (Kaplan 2020, 2022). Due to several reasons, such as the sector's general non-familiarity with and reluctance toward digital teaching and learning, this prediction did not materialize until the pandemic and its associated lockdowns compelling the majority of higher education establishments worldwide to switch to the digital sphere completely, in most cases overnight and in emergency mode (Kaplan 2021). Covid-19 might well have been the triggering event leading to the business school sector's disruption and significantly changing management education forever.

The pandemic increased alternative educational providers' prominence, and with it is changing the business of business schools. While many of these existed before the pandemic, these online alternatives have been often more appealing, less costly, and user-friendlier than what has been offered by traditional business schools. Moreover, the pandemic significantly raised the reach and visibility of ed and big tech in management education. Another alarming element of competition is the outcome shaped not only by these new arrivals, but also by fiercer rivalry among established business schools. Consequently, many management schools' leadership teams feel compelled to manage their institutions even more as for-profit businesses, thus accentuating a trend that has existed for some time. So where do we place the cursor on this school-to-business continuum in this new management education landscape? To better comprehend where business schools should position themselves in this judgment call, a detailed look at their revenues, and particularly cost structure, is proposed, completing the Competition-Cursor-Cost triangle.

2.1   Competition: Alarmingly Augmenting

Business schools are used to competition, fighting to attract the best professors and the brightest students destined for greatness. The desire to earn various accreditations and climb to the top of prestigious league rankings has likewise intensified rivalry (Guillotin and Mangematin 2015; Prasad, Segarra, and Villanueva 2019). Globalization trends in higher education did the same, with the market witnessing several noteworthy financial struggles, acquisitions, and mergers (Schlegelmilch 2020). At the same time, while both globalization and the quest for accreditations and ranking positions strengthened competition between business schools, they have also established high barriers for potential new entrants, notably regarding national and international accreditation bodies. The sector's digital transformation, however, among other effects, has opened competition to new alternative players and eased their entry into the business of management education (Kaplan 2020).

One group of such new entrants comes from the edtech sector, which increasingly raises serious competitors to established business schools

(Kaplan 2020, 2021, 2022). Take ThePowerMBA, a Spanish startup established in 2017, and its self-declared goal to revolutionize the worldwide MBA market. Essentially ThePowerMBA imitated and professionalized what Laurie Pickard (2017), a graduate of Temple University's Department of Geography, did on her own in 2016. Instead of applying to business school, Pickard, who had the ideal profile of an MBA candidate, decided to customize her self-designed MBA curriculum by enrolling in several of the world's most prestigious universities' MOOCs. She considered the top programs too costly, at least regarding her objectives and motivations for earning an MBA: she wanted to learn about business, not meet people or chase networks with fellow participants worldwide. Pickard saved thousands of dollars by spending less than $1,000 for her self-designed MBA. She earned the same academic credits, almost for free, as she would have by enrolling in Harvard, Wharton, or Yale. In addition, she could pick her classes from several institutions, i.e., attend the finance course at Wharton and the marketing one at Kellogg, both known for their respective world-class expertise in these disciplines. By now, more people seek to follow in Pickard's footsteps: ThePowerMBA enrolls approximately 25,000 yearly in their online, unaccredited, MBA certificate, costing around $1,000.

While the job market will decide whether such unofficial coursework will be considered equivalent to a university degree, the initial examples coming from big tech indicate a positive result. Similar to corporate universities (Nixon and Helms 2002), themselves intensifying competition, search engine titan Google launched its Career Certificates at the outbreak of Covid-19 (Schroeder 2022). These certificates enable participants to learn the currently in-demand professions of, e.g., project manager, data analyst, or digital marketer, in only three to six months, and for a couple of hundred dollars, just a fraction of business school tuition. Moreover, Google offers 100,000 scholarships. Most importantly, Google's hiring policy considers the successful completion of its Career Certificate as being equivalent to any four-year undergraduate degree. Graduates who do not wish to be employed by Google may apply at any of Google's 150 partner companies, including Walmart, BestBuy, and Bank of America. Other big tech giants, such as Microsoft's LinkedIn, also exhibit a growing interest in continuous education. Such a development's disruptive potential is undeniable.

Not only do new entrants increase competition, but rivalry is also on the rise within established business schools. Due to digital course offerings, geographically distant higher education institutions that previously may not have been counted among a given business school's direct competitors suddenly got very close, with the online sphere being just a click away. The prevalence of digital offerings has skyrocketed, and even more importantly, the number of those accustomed to working and learning online has as well. Why attend a course offered by an institution in your own country or state if you can just as well take digital classes at Harvard, Oxbridge, or Stanford? In the future, obtaining an online degree from a prestigious business schools might be considered equivalent to an on-campus program at a lesser-known institution. Students can thus avoid travel and housing costs. Indeed, some of the top institutions, such as Princeton University, have radically lowered their prices for their online programs, rendering this option even more appealing (Gallagher and Palmer 2020).

A fiercer competitive landscape leads to financial pressure exacerbated by rising costs due to, among others, tougher requirements from accreditors and league tables. Moreover, funding from public and private sources appears to be on the decline (Kaplan 2021). To counterbalance these phenomena, several solutions are applied. Cornell University, for example, decided to combine its Graduate School of Management, the School of Applied Economics and Management, and its world-famous School of Hotel Administration into the Cornell College of Business in hopes of consequent efficiencies and synergies (Peters, Smith, and Thomas 2018). Moreover, longstanding and highly ranked business schools have increased their enrollment and consequent market shares, leaving even fewer students for lower-tier schools, and thereby increasing the pressure on the latter. Likewise, not only business schools but higher education in general is on the warpath for the ever-elusive funding (Kaplan 2022). Consequently, several non-management institutions considering offering management education to increase their bottom line have opened up business schools within their structures, mimicking collegiate university structures where management schools (are compelled to) transfer some of their revenues to other disciplines and academic departments. An example thereof is Sciences Po Paris, traditionally focused on liberal arts and particularly political science, which in 2016 opened its School of Innovation and Management (Kaplan 2018). Such new schools at traditional non-management institutions further increase competition and pressure on the already increasingly saturated market of business education.

Finally, there is an ultimate source of increased competition, certainly prompting mention here, but also important to have on one's screen. Think about it: many people who seek to learn something new rapidly or need to get trained in something crucial to their job, often turn to neither a traditional nor a non-traditional educational provider, but simply follow a YouTube tutorial or engage in a quick Google or (future) ChatGPT search. For them, a three-to-five-minute YouTube video seems to adequately deliver the information, if not the knowledge, needed. On the instructional side, we're mostly talking about individuals without any particular academic background, who independently provide classes on, e.g., public speaking, investing in cryptocurrencies, or how one optimally can promote one's business in the metaverse. Millions of views "prove" their success. Mobile devices provide instant access to these "knowledge" sources, free of charge and recipe-like in their direct applicability. While they may not constitute competition for business schools (yet), in the longer run, we should not underestimate the fact that many potential learners consciously or unconsciously, consider such "training", provided by self-proclaimed educators and pedagogues, a legitimate alternative to sitting for hours in either a virtual or brick-and-mortar classroom.

2.2 Cursor: Business vs. School

Business schools have always been more open to business ethos and practices than other higher education disciplines. The opposite would be surprising given that these are the core of a business school's teaching. On the one hand, business schools are considered not-for-profit entities, producing knowledge, participating in social discourse, and educating future leaders in management and entrepreneurship. On the other hand, they can behave like companies and for-profit organizations, focusing on revenue and generation of margins (Pucciarelli and Kaplan 2016, 2017, 2019). To put it differently, we can ask whether a business school is better off being considered a school or a business. Where should we place the cursor on this continuum? From a historical viewpoint, the answer is quite straightforward: business schools at their inception were established as pure vocationally oriented trade schools. The aim was to train students as future leaders and obtain the best careers; it was not about gaining market share, let alone profits. In some business schools, however, the business side has taken over and become almost an obsession, with budgets invested in pedagogical quality and academics kept at a minimum (Peters, Smith, and Thomas 2018).

One could argue that with the uncertainty and complexity defining today's competitive business school landscape, deans and other leadership have no choice but to run a business school like a company. Yet I would affirm the opposite: the sector's digitalization leads to the entry of non-traditional, non-academic educational providers, be they private organizations or belonging to corporations. A strong positioning for established business schools is to differentiate themselves from those players, and to uphold academics over business affairs. Such prioritization, in addition to further measures, will strengthen business schools' edge. One of the core characteristics of higher education is to be a public good (Nedbalová, Greenacre, and Schulz 2014). By placing the cursor too far toward private business, business schools significantly weaken their public-good nature, and thus implicitly exit the higher education sector. In 2013, Prof. Robert Simons of Harvard Business School simply but most effectually declared, "The business of business schools is teaching business" (p. 31).

While pedagogy and students' personal development should be a top priority, business schools' budgets must be deployed efficaciously for the student good. Management theories and best practices should be part of business schools' operations precisely because of their being a business school. How can this be achieved? Simply by asking whether a given budget allocation will best enable students' becoming well-trained highly-qualified managers and entrepreneurs. This involves academic affairs and pedagogy, of course, but also personal development training likely provided by the business schools' career service, or any other experience that helps a student succeed in her future career. While budgets should be allocated to create value for all stakeholders of a business school, they ultimately should serve above all the students, with student-centricity having become of the essence in the digital era and its competitive landscape.

To illustrate this in more detail, take the example of online teaching. Currently, a pressing question is: what courses should be delivered online, and what courses should be taught offline? Instead of looking at costs and potential savings, we unsurprisingly should first consider what is the optimal solution between fully online, fully offline, or a hybrid format, pedagogically speaking. The answer should be the choice of action, with perhaps one possible exception (cf. Figure 2.1): imagine that the online course would cost half (€20k) of what it would cost to teach the course live (€40k), due to, e.g., offline classes not having to be taught several times in parallel. Imagine further that the offline course is only slightly better pedagogically than the online version. In this case, live instruction versus online instruction would result in only a small increment in value for the students (€80k vs. €70k). Now imagine taking the gain in budget resulting from providing the course online (€40k–€20k = €20k) and investing it elsewhere, e.g., the school's career service (€20k+€20k = €40k), through which this service's value increment could be doubled (from €30k to €60k). The new budget allocation would therefore lead to a much higher total value (€130k) for the student than would the previous allocation (€110k), while total cost is held constant at €60k. Note that both the academic coursework and the career service help students develop to become great managers and entrepreneurs. In brief, a business school should be about quality maximization (as seen from the students' point of view), not profit maximization.

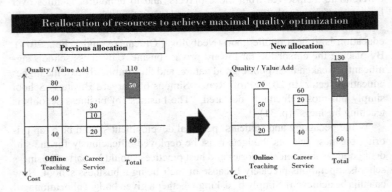

Figure 2.1 Quality Optimization vs. Profit Maximization

Such an approach to budget allocation may prompt several questions: for example, is it in the best interest of students to hire a high-salaried professor who publishes in the top journals? Maybe so, as publications help institutions to gain reputation and prestige. Or perhaps this would-be salary would better be invested in another domain. Is it in the best interest of students to invest massively in the university's physical plant? Maybe so, maybe not. If I asked my ESCP students in Paris what their preferred space was on campus, they would most likely cite a hallway in some basement where they organize their student societies. Aesthetically not the nicest location, but they love it. I am not suggesting that attractive real estate is not preferable; I do suggest that when making such decisions, the guiding principle should be quality optimization, which leads to an increased graduate employability and the best possible, most fulfilling and gratifying careers for alums. While not pretending that it is always easy to know what is in the best interest of students and what exactly results in quality optimization for them, it should at least underlie the business school leadership's applied line of thinking.

2.3   Cost: Choice and Complexity

To understand the business of business schools, it is helpful to have a look into their cost and revenue structures. To do so is not an easy task, due to the large variance therein. Keeping in mind that reality is far more complex, as a highly simplified illustration, Table 2.1 will serve to demonstrate a few general principles that should lend basic insight (d'Alessio and Avolio 2011). The starting point of this analysis will be a professor's cost, often considered the highest budget item on a business school's financial statement.

It is true that the cost of a professor can be high, especially at top, research-intensive institutions. Likewise, research can be pricy: the cost of one A+ article has been estimated at $400k (Byrne 2014). Table 2.1 makes some assumptions concerning a professor's cost, annual time spent on research, the average (A+) publication output annually achieved, and the number of an article's co-authors. While quantitative indicators are applied here, it would be desirable to also add qualitative ones (cf. Chapter 4). While these numbers should be adapted to your context, the table indicates that one publication costs between $250k and $600k. Note that this table looks at averages, not individual cases. Imagine the specific case of a professor whose salary is $200k and devotes 50% of her time to research. Now imagine that this professor publishes one article every five years, together with two colleagues in the same situation. Such an example is not unrealistic. The cost of this article would amount impressive $1.5 million (cf. special case: Unproductive Research). Thus you need many additional students' tuition to finance such costs. In contrast, for highly productive researchers, an article's total cost could also be as low as $200k (cf. special case: Productive Research).

Table 2.1 Cost and revenue analysis: an illustration

	Research							Teaching						Marketing	
Professor Cost	Research Time Quota	Annual Cost of Professor Research	Annual Number of Articles	Cost of Article per Author	Number of Co-authors	Cost per Article	Annual Number Teaching Hours per Professor	Annual Tuition per Student	Number of Students in Program	Total Program Revenues	Program Annual Teaching Hours	Annual Teaching Revenue per Professor	Direct Marketing Cost per Student: tuition %	Direct Marketing Cost per Student: absolute
(1)	(2)	(3) =1*2	(4)	(5) =3/4	(6)	(7) =5*6	(8)	(9)	(10)	(11) =9*10	(12)	(13) =(11/12)*8	(14)	(15) =9*10*14
100,000	0.00	0	0.00	n.a.	n.a.	n.a.	400	5,000	300	1,500,000	400	1,500,000	1%	50
100,000	0.00	0	0.00	n.a.	n.a.	n.a.	350	10,000	300	3,000,000	400	2,625,000	2%	200
150,000	0.25	37,500	0.30	125,000	3	375,000	300	15,000	200	3,000,000	300	3,000,000	3%	450
150,000	0.25	37,500	0.30	125,000	2	250,000	250	20,000	200	4,000,000	300	3,333,333	4%	800
200,000	0.50	100,000	0.50	200,000	3	600,000	200	25,000	100	2,500,000	300	1,666,667	5%	1,250
200,000	0.50	100,000	0.50	200,000	2	400,000	150	30,000	100	3,000,000	300	1,500,000	7%	2,100
300,000	0.50	150,000	1.00	150,000	3	450,000	100	40,000	50	2,000,000	300	666,667	10%	4,000
300,000	0.75	225,000	1.00	225,000	3	450,000	75	50,000	50	2,500,000	300	625,000	12%	6,000
400,000	0.75	300,000	2.00	150,000	3	450,000	50	75,000	25	1,875,000	200	468,750	15%	11,250
400,000	0.75	300,000	2.00	150,000	2	300,000	25	100,000	25	2,500,000	200	312,500	20%	20,000

Special Cases

(1)	(2)	(3)	(4)	(5)	(6)	(7)		(8)	(9)	(10)	(12)	(13)
400,000	0.75	300,000	3	100,000	2	200,000	Productive Research	25	100,000	200	200	2,500,000
200,000	0.50	100,000	0.2	500,000	3	1,500,000	Unproductive Research	25	15,000	4,000	300	5,000,000

Productive Teaching: Offline
Productive Teaching: Online

Additional Cost Blocks

* **Branding**: achieved via, e.g., general institutional communications, research-based branding, or rankings and accreditations
* **Real Estate**: impacted by occupation rates and the ratio of online vs. offline teaching
* **Complexity**: generated via, e.g., multiplying of programs necessitating additional academic and non-academic staff

Yet, to be fair to professors, we also need to look at how much revenue a professor can generate. Taking into account the number of hours a professor has to teach, tuition costs, and the number of course hours in a respective program, puts a professor's yearly teaching revenue in a range between around $300k to $3.3 million. Moreover, many professors engage in additional teaching hours, i.e., actual revenues exceed these sums. To understand the table's logic, we need to consider that usually the most research-active professors have a very reduced annual teaching load. Moreover, they usually (should) teach in graduate programs (e.g., MBA or Executive MBA), which in most cases mean small class sizes, justifying higher tuition fees. There are exceptions to this rule: star researchers especially might point out that due to their popularity, they teach classes with 200+ high-tuition enrollees. Although only teaching 25 hours per year, such professors would generate revenues of $2.5 million (cf. special case: Productive Teaching: offline) for their university.

While revenues from graduate students are a lot higher, profitability does not necessarily follow the same direction. Executive education participants demand better food plans, more exciting study trips, and generally a significantly higher service level than do undergraduate students. Moreover, program structure is more complex, with more elective course options and choices. Finally, or rather initially, before you teach students, you need to attract them, i.e., marketing expenditure represents an important budgetary item in a business school. Less costly and less advanced programs usually spend a lower percentage of tuition on marketing. Applying so-called direct marketing expenditures creates costs for, e.g., mailings, LinkedIn in-mails, or tradeshow presences (Roberts and Berger 1989), in the range of 1% to 20% of tuition. Absolute cost to attract one student would therefore range from $50 to $20,000.

Alongside direct marketing, business schools also engage in branding (cf. Chapter 7; Hemsley-Brown and Goonawardana 2007) via media or general communications promoting the entire institution. Equal in importance to direct marketing (actually complementing it), branding affects application numbers only indirectly. Imagine that you receive an email featuring a business school with which you're not familiar, whose program sounds interesting. Most likely, you'll do a quick search to find out about this institution, i.e., you want to assure yourself that this school is reputable and has a relatively strong brand. Research represents a good communications source, so that the high cost of research-active professors might be justified via their publications' branding potential, but if and only if their research is of broad media interest (cf. Chapter 4), which is rather rarely the case (Bennis and O'Toole (2005).

Next to research, powerful branding can be achieved via top rankings, or prestigious accreditations (Kaplan and Pucciarelli 2016). Particularly their indirect costs, generated by rankings' and accreditations' demanding requirements and standards, weigh heavily on an institution's budget. For example, to be considered, in many cases a business school needs to prove that a significant share of course hours (up to 50%) is taught by research-active professors. Schools where faculty is not engaged in research (cf. first two lines of Table 2.1), while less costly, are usually also not eligible for many of the prestigious league tables and accreditation bodies (cf. Chapter 6).

Room, i.e., real estate, is a further important cost factor. Buildings are costly, especially since too often they have low occupancy, notably during summer. To raise occupancy rates during this period, some business schools provide summer programs for high schoolers to get a taste of university and campus life. Instead of increasing occupancy, one could also pursue a strategy of reducing space on the theory that buildings will soon belong to the past, with online teaching overtaking them.

Yet, we should not forget that online programs generate less tuition than their offline or hybrid versions. Top institutions, such as aforementioned Princeton, significantly lowered their tuition for online degrees during the pandemic (Gallagher and Palmer 2020). A productive online instructor can teach thousands of students via an asynchronous digital course, for example. A star professor who teaches 4,000 (medium tuition-paying) students would generate revenues of $5 million (cf. special case: Productive Teaching: online). Obviously, such a professor would ask for more than their allotted teaching load, probably applying some coefficient to the teaching hours, which would increase cost. Additionally, such a course might demand several teaching assistants and further personnel. Moreover, real estate is of high importance for networking and community building. Especially in times of increased rivalry, alums' attachment to their alma mater will increasingly become vital (cf. Chapter 8; Kaplan 2021, 2022).

Finally, we haven't yet addressed the most important cost block and driver, at least to me. In my deanship experience, this element is of such high relevance that I titled this chapter's section accordingly. Too much choice and complexity are certainly the most hidden and difficult budget lines for which to detect a cost factor. Organizational complexity has significantly increased over the years. Whereas most business schools used to have only a couple of degree programs, now some offerings have tripled or quadrupled in volume. The aim of this increase is to provide programs that are better adapted to potential applicants, i.e., applying the marketing principle of segmentation and targeting (Kotler 1997). While such an approach usually leads to more appealing programs for specific targets, and hopefully to an overall increase in enrollment, on the downside, it also means a lot more work for business schools, demanding a lot more HR: marketing collateral needs to be adapted, every single program accredited, curricula and syllabi designed, and study trips and other events organized. Obviously, we can and should opt for modular structures with high synergies and efficiencies between the multitude of programs, provided overall academic quality remains high. However, program offerings grow gradually, and such synergies are often missed. This represents only one of several examples wherein complexity has entered business schools. To detect complexity with the aim of significantly reducing it, we need to take a close look at operations and processes. My experience tells me that doing so is definitely worth it.

References

Bennis W. G., O'Toole J. (2005) How business schools lost their way. *Harvard Business Review, 83*(5), 96–104.

Byrne J. A. (2014) Cost of an academic article: $400K, poets & quants. July 16, available online at https://poetsandquants.com/2014/07/16/the-shockingly-high -cost-of-an-academic-article-400k/.

D'Alessio F. A., Avolio B. (2011) Business schools and resources constraints: A task for deans? Or magicians? *Research in Higher Education Journal, 13.* Available online at www.aabri.com/manuscripts/11912.pdf.

Datar S., Garvin D. A., Cullen P. G. (2010) *Rethinking the MBA: Business education at a crossroads.* Harvard Business Press.

Eckardt J., Wetherbe J. C. (2014) Making business school research more relevant. *Harvard Business Review,* December 24.

Gallagher S., Palmer J. (2020) *The pandemic pushed universities online. The change was long overdue.* Harvard Business Publishing, September 30, available online at https://hbsp.harvard.edu/inspiring-minds/the-pandemic-pushed-universities -online-the-change-was-long-overdue.

Ghoshal S. (2005) Bad management theories are destroying good management practices. *Academy of Management Learning & Education, 4*(1), 75–91.

Glick W., Tsui A., Davis G. (2018) The moral dilemma of business research. *AACSB BizEd,* May 2, 32–37.

Guillotin B., Mangematin V. (2015) Internationalization strategies of business schools: How flat is the world? *Thunderbird International Business Review, 57*(5), 343–357.

Hemsley-Brown J., Goonawardana S. (2007) Brand harmonization in the international higher education market. Journal of Business Research, *60*(9), 942–948.

Jack A. (2020) Academic focus limits business schools' contribution to society. *Financial Times,* February 24.

Kaplan A. (2014) European Management and European Business Schools: Insights from the history of business schools. *European Management Journal, 32*(4), 529–534.

Kaplan A. (2017) Academia goes social media: MOOC, SPOC, SMOC, and SSOC: The digital transformation of higher education institutions and universities. In B. Rishi and S. Bandyopadhyay (eds.), *Contemporary issues in social media marketing.* London: Routledge.

Kaplan A. (2018) "A School is a Building that Has 4 Walls – with Tomorrow Inside": Toward the reinvention of the business school. *Business Horizons, 61*(4), 599–608.

Kaplan A. (2020) Universities, be aware: Start-Ups strip away your glory: About EdTech's potential take-over of the higher education sector. efmdglobal.org, May 11, 2020, available online at https://blog.efmdglobal.org/2020/05/11/universities -be-aware-start-ups-strip-away-your-glory/.

Kaplan A. (2021) *Higher education at the crossroads of disruption: The university of the 21ˢᵗ century - Great debates in higher education.* Emerald Publishing.

Kaplan A. (2022) *Digital transformation and disruption of higher education.* Cambridge University Press.

Kaplan A., Haenlein M. (2016) Higher education and the digital revolution: MOOCs, SPOCs, Social Media, and the Cookie Monster. *Business Horizons, 59*(4), 441–450.

Kaplan A., Pucciarelli F. (2016) Contemporary challenges in higher education: Three E's for education: Enhance, embrace, expand. *IAU Horizons*, International Universities Bureau of the United Nations, *21*(4), 25–26.

Khurana R., Spender J.-C. (2012) Herbert A. Simon on what ails business schools: More than 'a problem in organization design'. *Journal of Management Studies 49*(3), 619–639.

Kotler P. (1997) *Marketing management analysis, planning, implementation, and control.* Prentice Hall International.

Locke R. R., Spender J.-C. (2011) *Confronting managerialism: How the business elite and their schools threw our lives out of balance.* Zed Books.

Mintzberg H. (2004) *Managers, not MBAs: A hard look at the soft practice of managing and management development.* Berrett-Koehler.

Nedbalová E., Greenacre L., Schulz J. (2014) UK higher education viewed through the marketization and marketing lenses. *Journal of Marketing for Higher Education, 24*(2), 178–195.

Nixon J. C., Helms M. M. (2002) Corporate universities vs higher education institutions. *Industrial and Commercial Training, 34*(4), 144–150.

Pappano L. (2012) The year of the MOOC. *New York Times*, November 2.

Parker M. (2018) *Shut down the business school: What's wrong with management education?* London: Pluto Press.

Peters K., Smith R. R., Thomas H. (2018) *Rethinking the business models of business schools: A critical review and change agenda for the future.* Emerald Publishing.

Pickard L. (2017) *Don't pay for your MBA: The faster, cheaper, better way to get the business education you need.* AMACOM.

Prasad A., Segarra P., Villanueva C. E. (2019) Academic life under institutional pressures for AACSB accreditation: Insights from faculty members in Mexican business schools. *Studies in Higher Education, 44*(9), 1605–1618.

Pucciarelli F., Kaplan A. (2016) Competition and strategy in higher education: Managing complexity and uncertainty. *Business Horizons, 59*(3), 311–320.

Pucciarelli F., Kaplan A. (2017) Le Università Europee oggi: Sfide e nuove strategie. *Economia & Management*, gennaio/febbraio, *1*, 85–95.

Pucciarelli F., Kaplan A. (2019) Competition in higher education. In B. Nguyen, T. C. Melewar, & J. Hemsley-Brown (eds.), *Strategic brand management in higher education.* Routledge.

Pucciarelli F., Kaplan A. (2022) A transition to a hybrid teaching model as a step forward toward responsible management education? *Journal of Global Responsibility, 3*(1), 7–20.

Roberts, M. L., Berger P. D. (1989) *Direct marketing management.* Prentice Hall.

RRBM Network (2022) Vision 2030, Responsible research in business & management network, https://www.rrbm.network/position-paper/vision-2030/.

Schlegelmilch B. B. (2020) Why business schools need radical innovations: Drivers and development trajectories. *Journal of Marketing Education, 42*(2), 93–107.

Schroeder R. (2022) Google career certificates: Heralding the future. *Inside Higher Ed*, March 2, available online at: https://www.insidehighered.com/digital-learning /blogs/online-trending-now/google-career-certificates-heralding-future.

Shapiro D. L., Kirkman B. (2018) It's time to make business school research more relevant. July 19, *Harvard Business Review*.

Simons R. (2013) The business of business schools: Restoring a focus on competing to win. *Capitalism and Society, 8*(1), Art. 2.

Wilson D. C., Thomas H. (2012) Challenges and criticisms: The legitimacy of the business of business schools: What's the future? *Journal of Management Development, 31*(4), 368–376.

3 Business Schools' Deep Dive into Digital Disruption

Due to the sector's digital transformation, business schools are facing a period of profound change (Kaplan 2021c). Edtech, such as the Spanish startup ThePowerMBA or French career center platform JobTeaser; and big tech alternative educational providers such as Microsoft's LinkedIn Learning or Facebook aka Meta's Metaverse Academy, are now part of the competitive landscape. Accordingly, business schools must think of ways to protect themselves from such new rivalry or devise solutions for cooperation and coexistence (Kaplan 2020a).

While the pandemic was not experienced uniformly across the globe, and its effects on specific higher education markets were uneven, it did trigger online teaching and its acceleration in an unprecedented manner (Mazurek 2022; Sporn 2022). Teaching a program completely on site without any online elements no longer makes sense, as more and more modules are delivered digitally in the form of MOOCs, SPOCs, SMOCs, and SSOCs (Kaplan and Haenlein 2016; Kaplan 2017). Consequently, a certain share of business schools' programs will be taught digitally. Hopefully, business schools will remember what they are teaching, i.e., not make the mistake that other sectors have made, of simply transferring their offline products and services into the digital sphere without adjusting to its specificities.

The digitalization of the business school environment, and of academia generally, is welcomed differingly by various institutions. While some acknowledge potential disruption, others feel such assertions are exaggerated. An analysis of ed and big tech's strengths and assets, many mindsets having shifted during the pandemic, sheds light on this issue, which dominates many schools' Board of Directors meetings as well as heated debates among higher education experts. How should business schools confront digital transformation, not to mention digital disruption? Advances in artificial intelligence, the application of big data to higher education, and the future metaverse are just some of the various opportunities to consider. What parts of business education should be digitalized, and what should remain offline? Pedagogical innovation and the simplicity of sensemaking are the defining drivers thereof, and serve as a line of argumentation to answering this question. One even could predict and defend a new research < > teaching paradigm, shifting some of a

DOI: 10.4324/9781003343509-3

school's current focus on research back to teaching and pedagogical quality. Ultimately, professors might have to consider imitating celebrities such as Greta Garbo, Britney Spears, and Kendall Jenner.

3.1   Moving Many Mindsets

Beyond accelerating higher education's digital transformation and business schools' entry into their partly-virtual era (Murphy, Inesto, and Scanlon 2022), the pandemic, more importantly, moved many mindsets concerning online education (Kaplan 2021 a,b,c). During the pandemic lockdowns, many experienced and learned to appreciate online education for the first time. They enrolled in online programs of non-traditional academic institutions that were more user-friendly and appealing than those of established management schools. In contrast to longer, more extended, and relatively costly course-work at business schools, the digital modular offering is much cheaper and more compact in program duration. When confronted with the danger coming from ed and big tech entrants, recurrently, management schools defend themselves, stating that attending business school is not only about studying academic content, but also extends services such as networking and career counseling. In this section, we'll look at the various reasons students enroll in business school and how alternative providers enter this market and position themselves (Kaplan 2020a, b). Notably, the aforementioned ThePowerMBA, providing a non-accredited, €999 online MBA program, will serve as a prime example.

In most cases, students seek to enroll in a business school with strong notoriety and brand – which many do – significantly facilitating the subsequent job search. One might believe it difficult for startups such as ThePowerMBA to compete with such brand strength. By the same token, L'Oréal and General Electric did not expect Google to overtake them in their brand value, relatively shortly after its establishment on September 4, 1989. And yet it did. The tech giants have become students' preferred employers, pushing companies such as Coca-Cola or consultancies McKinsey, BCG, or Bain off the podium. Google Certificates, LinkedIn Learning, or the Metaverse Academy are no longer unknown; they've rapidly increased their brand equity and have themselves strong mother brands in the background partly included in their names. ThePowerMBA, created in 2017, has already expanded its enrollment by 2,000 – not per year, but rather per month. In a decade, this will mean approximately half a million people having direct contact with the brand. Future students, increasingly liberated from peer pressure and parental decision power, might feel freer to make unconventional decisions and choose innovativeness and creativity over tradition and conventional brand power.

Next to notoriety, students look to obtain an official degree and diploma. Indeed, business schools often claim to be the unique issuers of accredited management degrees, as ed and big tech players do not (yet) issue official certification. There are exceptions, such as the Berlin-based Code University, which achieved the privilege of octroying state-accredited diplomas only a couple of years after its establishment. Looking at ThePowerMBA shows how non-accreditation even can be framed as an advantage, with their resisting offering recognized degrees:

> NO, we don't, and we don't want to. For years we were told that to get to "the top", you need a Master's degree. Perhaps this was true ten years ago, but nowadays, this idea is obsolete. Official MBAs must adhere to specific syllabi that make learning less flexible. In contrast, we update our content monthly; it's one of our main value propositions. Nonetheless, thanks to a content agreement with Harvard Business Publishing Education, you will receive a Harvard ManageMentor® certificate upon completing any of our programs
>
> (ThePowerMBA 2022)

This agility-vs.-outdatedness argument might convince at least a few potential enrollees. If not, a certificate labeled "Harvard" just might.

Business schools not only pride themselves on having international labels and degree-awarding powers, but also consider themselves experts in instruction and pedagogy. ThePowerMBA, however, appears unimpressed by business schools' teaching quality delivered by experienced pedagogues, and counters with their innovative pedagogical approach implemented through renowned practitioners.

> Our methodology combines 15-minute online classes with which you can learn at your own pace from any device and place, with live webinars with our instructors, where you will have the opportunity to expand your knowledge, solve questions, spark debates and share the experience in real time with …fellow students in each program. […] Some of the successful figures that you are going to find in our programs are: Marc Randolph (co-founder of Netflix), Uri Levine (founder of Waze), Chris Barton (founder of Shazam), Randi Zuckerberg (CEO and founder of Zuckerberg Media), and Daniel Lamarre (CEO of Cirque du Soleil)
>
> (ThePowerMBA 2022)

Knowing how much students like listening to practitioners, and exposing them to such known names, is a strong selling argument for ThePowerMBA.

Joining networks of like-minded and successful alumni is another reason that students enroll in business school. However, LinkedIn illustrates that the internet increasingly provides ways to cultivate one's network, with LinkedIn having become the biggest competitor of any business school's alumni association. ThePowerMBA also recognizes the importance of networks and networking:

> What started as a disruptive business school has quickly grown into a movement with over 80,000 students, in over 100 countries around the world, more than 400 networking events per year, and hundreds of social communities. We are an online business school, but we don't want to miss the opportunity to network, connect, and share experiences with people in the same situation than we are in. That's why we organize virtual networking events almost every week that you can attend for free. In addition, we organize more than 400 face-to-face networking events per year all over the world (Spain, Mexico, USA, Germany, etc.)
>
> (ThePowerMBA 2022)

Traditional business schools pride themselves in having a high-quality alumni community. New entrants counter with extremely high-quantity networks. The two are not mutually exclusive.

Finally, the most salient reason for students enrolling in business school is finding satisfactory employment. Business schools rationalize their (ever-rising) tuition by assuring their students that they will find their (high-paid) dream jobs after graduation due to, inter alia, the institution's competent career service teams. However, career services are increasingly outsourced to edtech career service platforms such as the aforementioned JobTeaser (Knight, Staunton, and Healy 2022), constituting yet another threat. Companies prefer to recruit preselected students taught a certain set of competencies from a limited number of high-profile business schools. Edtech replaces preselection with post-matching: advanced information technology enables analysis of a multitude of data, enabling employers to identify the ideal employer < > student match. LinkedIn, for example, collects millions of data points, knows what jobs are on offer and in demand, and what qualifications its users have. ThePowerMBA's FAQ section summarizes this phenomenon:

> We realized that traditional job boards don't work. That's why we have implemented a UNIQUE application process for candidates based on Big Data and Artificial Intelligence. This allows us to analyze your profile and get to know you from a 360° perspective so that we can show you the positions that suit you best. We have established connections and relationships with the best companies in the country that trust us to send us their job offers, and, in turn, we send them qualified and pre-filtered candidates for the position. These companies include, among many others, … Google, Microsoft, Accenture, Roche, or [*sic*] Coca-Cola
>
> (ThePowerMBA 2022)

Table 3.1 Competitiveness of the ed and big tech sector

	Traditional Business Schools		Ed and Big Tech Alternatives
Offering	Extended and expensive	vs	Compact and cheap
Notoriety	Established brands		Innovative newcomers
Labeling	Approval of accreditation		Agility of non-accreditation
Instruction	Experienced pedagogues		Renowned practitioners
Network	High-quality		High-quantity
Employment	Preselection		Post-matching

I am well aware that a FAQ also serves the purpose of marketing and communications, and that we all seek to present ourselves in the best light, and ThePowerMBA is no different. Nonetheless, ThePowerMBA's arguments have been convincing enough for me to join them as a regular, paying enrollee, one reason for which was to see how their FAQs check out in reality. I found that ed and big tech still have a long way to go to reach the level of established business schools. Nonetheless, a recent study by CarringtonCrisp revealed that nearly 40 percent of respondents would consider pursuing their studies with alternative educational providers such as Coursera, Quantic, or ThePower MBA instead of enrolling in a traditional MBA program (Bisoux 2022). Well-established schools should start to clearly position themselves and showcase their advantages and value proposition in contrast to alternatives increasingly available in the management education market. Analogously, many silent picture stars got caught by surprise when sound was added to the movies. Only a few managed the transition successfully, Greta Garbo being one of them. Business schools should be keen to follow her favorable transition into the "talkie" era.

3.2 Simplicity of Sense-Making

"Online simply must make sense" (Kaplan 2021a). That sentence should be the guiding principle when deciding what elements of a course or program should be taught online and what is better provided offline. Easier said than done, especially as the borders between the real and the virtual worlds increasingly blur, affected by AI progress, big data, virtual reality, and the metaverse, as well as augmented reality and holographs (Malagocka, Mazurek, and Kaplan 2022). What does not make sense is to spout cut-and-dried statements such as "Every second session should be done online," "We don't have enough physical space; thus let's move more courses online," or "We need to show that we're advanced in the digital transformation, therefore let's be the first to move into the metaverse." Each environment – both virtual and live – has its advantages and drawbacks (Seeletso 2022, Shcheglova, Vilkova, and Dremova 2022). This recognition must underlay the spirit and mindset of business schools' approach and digitalization strategies.

One advantage of, e.g., applying AI to learning is the pedagogical customization potential, i.e., tailoring both the level and speed of instruction to the background and requirements of the learner, or what is known as "adaptive learning." Think of an online language learning program: artificial intelligence will detect the learner's language skills and weak and strong spots, and accordingly adapt the exercises and questions that it assigns them. Likewise, AI can also serve to improve offline courses. Learning analytics – in simple terms, the big data of higher education – can be used by faculty to monitor students' progress and evaluate the pedagogical approach, course content, teaching resources, and so forth. Likewise, students themselves may use such analytics for self-evaluation purposes (Pucciarelli and Cobo-Benita 2022).

AI moreover supports academic and non-academic staff in their routine commitments, thereby freeing up their time for higher-value tasks (Kaplan 2022a, c). Think of Jill Watson, Georgia Tech's chatbot, responding to multiple recurring student questions (McFarland 2016). Imagine AI-driven machines grading student essays and exam papers, imitating an instructor's grading style within less than one percentage point disparity (Zawacki-Richter et al. 2019). Imagine AI-supported admissions systems, considering a candidate's way of interacting with the university's website or e-mail exchange, assessing her likelihood of enrollment, and successfully completing the program. The application of AI in higher education certainly makes sense. However, there are also limitations. Artificial intelligence, for example, is able to detect a learner's emotional state (on- and offline) via cameras and facial expression analysis (Liesaputra and Ott 2022), which could provide faculty with information concerning the individual's or group's attention level, degree of comprehension, and the like. Already applied in China, such an approach, however, is questionable in the light of students' data protection and right to privacy (Haenlein, Huang, and Kaplan 2022; Kaplan and Haenlein 2019, 2020).

Also, the future metaverse (Kaplan and Haenlein 2010a; Kaplan and Haenlein 2009 a,b,c) is expected to massively impact higher education and business schools, providing an entirely new environment in which to study. Students will immerse in the metaverse to participate in courses, work on group assignments, or join extracurriculars. Several universities and business schools have already created virtual campuses where students in the form of avatars can study, meet, and mingle. There are already virtual campus tours for potential candidates who want to get a feel for a given institution. Not only could the metaverse provide a new environment in which to teach and learn, but it could also improve and augment the learning process itself (Butson and O'Callahan 2022).

Let's say that you want to learn about negotiation techniques. The metaverse would enable you to beam yourself right into the middle of a Turkish bazaar and immerse yourself in the basics of negotiation between a merchant and a tourist seeking a bargain. Or, you want to learn about the functioning of a stock exchange: why not directly observe stock traders – avatars, I mean – in a digital version of Wall Street? Or instead of physically going on a start-up safari tour in Berlin, Hamburg, Lisbon, or Paris, you could do so in the metaverse hopping from one virtual startup to another, from the comfort of home and wearing your VR headset, gloves, and body suit. Only our imagination limits the potential applications. While the deployment of the metaverse for higher education purposes will definitely make sense in the future, for the moment the technology is not completely there yet. Nonetheless, it certainly makes sense for every business school student to be exposed at least once to such an immersive virtual environment, to get used to what it will mean to work and navigate therein.

These new technologies and platforms – or virtual worlds – will all need to be applied to optimize academic quality. Synchronous online classes via Zoom or someday in the metaverse will serve students with health or mobility issues, or who cannot afford commuting or living costs away from home, or merely for sustainability reasons. Well-designed asynchronous online modules might make sense for learning facts and pure knowledge instead of professors repeatedly delivering the same material in the lecture hall, thereby enabling them to use their time more productively. Also, during a semester abroad or internships, when the home institution's contact with students is less regular, online meetings might foster a sense of connection. Instead of guest lecturers flying expensively and unsustainably around the world, augmented-reality holographic technology could be used to transport them into classrooms, with the possibility of transmitting such holograms to multiple sites simultaneously. Moreover, leaders in given fields might feel it easier to provide students with a glimpse of their daily work via videoconference or hologram, instead of taking half a day or more to go to a business school's campus.

Along with defying time and space limitations, the virtual sphere should also be used for pedagogical innovation to go beyond the simple replication of what is done offline. Academic curricula as we know them today might utterly change: programs could begin with an online period where adaptive learning brings individual students, potentially simultaneously working in a company, up to the same level. In the second phase, they could get together for live instruction, perhaps augmented by the virtual sphere, but enabling getting to know each other in person and engaging in a variety of networking activities. Finally, the program could finish with students working at a given company getting academic tutoring, online coaching, and sessions on personal development, in parallel. Additionally, such a program structure would be consistent with the increasing importance of continuous education and lifelong learning, preparing students for an integrative modus of working and learning over their entire professional lives.

In the future, human teachers might be replaced by AI-driven machines, holograms, bots, or humanoids. While this won't happen for a while (Haenlein and Kaplan 2019), you might be wrong in thinking that students will always prefer human instructors over artificially intelligent ones. In analogy, a study by the Center for the Governance of Change at Spain's IE University demonstrated that one-fourth of Europeans would prefer that AI-driven systems govern instead of human politicians, who might be extreme ideologically or tempted by corruption (Rubio et al., 2019). On the other hand, looking at the music industry might give one hope: although stars like Britney Spears (Kaplan and Haenlein 2012) exist in the format of MP3s and YouTube videos, her live concerts still sell out. Only the future will tell what exactly will happen and what is most efficient and sense-making. For the time being, however, the digital sphere is not the ideal format for all situations, subjects, and courses. Or, to end this section as it started: online simply must make sense (Kaplan 2021a).

3.3   Research < > Teaching Paradigm Shift

Throughout higher education history, research has gradually become the center of a professor's career, often at the expense of teaching (Kaplan 2014, 2018). To get a desirable position, those seeking careers in academia must publish in the "right" journals, starting with their PhD theses. To obtain tenure at a business school, in many cases only the number of publications in a select number of journals counts (Adler and Harzing 2009; Vermeulen 2005). Consequently, pedagogy and teaching quality are reduced to supporting roles; at some institutions, they don't play any role: teaching can be neglected, as "what happens in the classroom stays in the classroom." Poor evaluations by students is often blamed on being stricter in grading or more demanding in homework and workload than other instructors, which might be true, but is sometimes not.

However, with business schools' digital transformation, teaching quality becomes far more transparent and testable. Potential students can watch an institution's professors on YouTube or participate in one of their MOOCs. For the moment, only a minor share of professors can be evaluated thusly online, as not all of them are exposing themselves in asynchronous teaching modules. However, in the future, a similar phenomenon might occur as with job recruiters looking at applicants' social media presences before inviting them to interview. An applicant's not being findable on Facebook, Instagram, or LinkedIn might arouse suspicion. Likewise, faculty not visible online, including a presentation of their pedagogical competencies, might also arouse suspicion, with the result of a recruiter's moving on to the next applicant or potential student moving on to the next institution on her list. Moreover, one even could imagine the effect of a specific analysis of a certain course taught by a certain professor on a graduates' obtaining a certain job: more and more students put on their LinkedIn profiles the exact list of courses they took at business schools. AI then could use these (big) data sets to calculate whether a certain combination of courses leads to better chances of getting a desirable job.

Overall, the higher education sector's digitalization and new possibilities provided by advances in information technology might lead to a research < > teaching switch, i.e., a pedagogy < > science paradigm shift, restoring more importance to teaching, and less to research. Let's take the aforementioned discussion about AI-driven holograms and humanoid professors back a notch, and return to the current reality of MOOCs, SPOCs, and the like. It appears reasonable that more emphasis on online teaching will lead to the phenomenon of "star" (online) instructors, in the same way that the system of highly paid "star" researchers has resulted from business schools' increased focus on research (Neely, Tribunella, Tang, and Hull 2008).

Such a trend could prompt an entire pedagogy < > science paradigm shift with more balance between research and teaching. One could argue that star teachers have always existed, e.g., those who write bestselling textbooks (or books for a general audience) are always high profile. The difference, however, is that now students can not only read a professor's textbook, but truly experience his or her pedagogical qualities via, e.g., taking an online course and comparing it with what happens at one's home institution. As teaching becomes more visible and testable, business schools will need to invest in training their current faculty (Kaplan and Haenlein 2016). This is true especially for those research-active faculty members, recruited as such, who might need to become better teachers and pedagogues.

Not every faculty member has the potential to become a star (online) teacher, just as not everybody is made to be a star researcher, or a star at all. For the moment, we still consider humans to be the desired choice for teaching compared to robots or AI-produced holographic instructors. A good way to find out who tomorrow's "stars" will be is to search among your faculty who today receive above-average student evaluations. To successfully attract thousands of learners online, an instructor must be telegenic and exhibit charisma. Focusing more on tenured senior professors rather than newcomers might be wise. Becoming a celebrity takes effort, and schools should ensure that the newly risen star will remain loyal to the institution before investing important resources. Also note that competitors interested in "headhunting" a celebrity online teacher can be numerous, as not only rival business schools might fight for your star faculty, but so will corporations (Kaplan and Haenlein 2016).

Ultimately, professors increasingly need to be technophiles, as they will be expected to master the latest teaching technologies. They will need to integrate learning analytics that they obtain from the learning management systems (LMS) in place. They will need to be able to teach in the form of avatars or holograms. At some point, they might even be judged on their visibility online and their appeal to potential students and continuing education participants. Just as one looks at one's citation count on Google Research concerning professors' scientific impact, one might look at their number of followers on LinkedIn or other social media (Kaplan and Haenlein 2010b). Sound exaggerated? Perhaps. But as aforementioned, when I referred to (silent and sound) star Greta Garbo and pop princess Britney Spears, here, I'll draw an analogy to Kendall Jenner, modeling, and how the mannequin business has changed over time. Kendall Jenner is now the highest-paid supermodel. This might be due to her looks, work ethic, or other reasons. It might also be due to her visibility and popularity as a family member of the Kardashians, and her 250 million followers on Instagram. When attending a model casting, applicants must now provide the number of followers on their various social media accounts. This might also become true for professors and deans at some point: the more followers they have, the more they act as promotional tools and as their institution's (teaching) ambassadors.

References

Adler N. J., Harzing A. W. (2009) When knowledge wins: Transcending the sense and nonsense in academic rankings. *Academy of Management Learning & Education*, 8, 72–95.

Bisoux T. (2022) The latest surveys show that prospective students still value graduate management education, even as more prioritize flexibility and lifelong learning. *AACSB*, February 7, 2022, available online at https://www.aacsb.edu/insights/articles/2022/02/what-trends-are-shaping-business-education.

Butson R., O'Callahan K. (2022) Personal analytics in the science of learning. In A. Kaplan (ed.), *Digital transformation and disruption of higher education* (pp. 377–390). Cambridge University Press.

Haenlein M., Kaplan A. (2019) A brief history of AI: On the past, present, and future of artificial intelligence. *California Management Review*, 61(4), 5–14.

Haenlein M., Huang M.-H., Kaplan A. (2022) Business ethics in the era of artificial intelligence. Special Issue, *Journal of Business Ethics*.

Kaplan A. (2014) European Management and European Business Schools: Insights from the history of business schools. *European Management Journal*, 32(4), 529–534.

Kaplan A. (2017) Academia goes social media – MOOC, SPOC, SMOC, and SSOC: The digital transformation of higher education institutions and universities. In B. Rishi, S. Bandyopadhyay (eds.), *Contemporary Issues in Social Media Marketing*. Routledge.

Kaplan A. (2018) "A School is a Building that Has 4 Walls – with Tomorrow Inside": Toward the reinvention of the business school, *Business Horizons*, 61(4), 599–608.

Kaplan A. (2020) Universities, beware: Start-ups strip your glory: EdTech's potential takeover of the higher education sector. *efmdglobal.org*, May 11, 2020, available online at https://blog.efmdglobal.org/2020/05/11/universities-be-aware-start-ups-strip-away-your-glory/.

Kaplan A. (2021a) Business schools: Going digital simply must make sense! *efmdglobal .org*, January 5, 2021, available online at https://blog.efmdglobal.org/2021/01/05/business-schools-going-digital-simply-must-make-sense/.

Kaplan A. (2021b) *Higher education at the crossroads of disruption: The university of the 21ˢᵗ century – Great debates in higher education.* Emerald Publishing.

Kaplan A. (2021c) *Professionals need to keep their skills fresh. Will they turn to higher ed?* Harvard Business Publishing, September 17, 2021. Available online at https://www.hbsp.harvard.edu/inspiring-minds/professionals-need-to-keep-their -skills-fresh-will-they-turn-to-higher-ed/?ab=top_nav.

Kaplan A. (2022a) *Artificial intelligence, business, and civilization: Our fate made in machines.* Routledge.

Kaplan A. (2022b) *Digital Transformation and Disruption of Higher Education.* Cambridge University Press.

Kaplan A. (2022c) Innovation in artificial intelligence: Illustrations in academia, apparel, and the arts. *Oxford Research Encyclopedia of Business and Management.* Oxford University Press.

Kaplan A., Haenlein M. (2009a) Consumer use and business potential of virtual worlds: The case of Second Life. *International Journal on Media Management, 11*(3/4), 93–101.

Kaplan A., Haenlein M. (2009b) Consumers, companies, and virtual social worlds: A qualitative analysis of Second Life. *Advances in Consumer Research, 36*(1), 873–874.

Kaplan A., Haenlein M. (2009c) The fairyland of Second Life: About virtual social worlds and how to use them. *Business Horizons, 52*(6), 563–572.

Kaplan A., Haelein M. (2010a) Mondes virtuels : Retour au realism. *Expansion Management Review, 138*(Septembre), 90–102.

Kaplan A., Haenlein M. (2010b) Uitdagingen en kansen rond social media. *Management Executive, 8*(3), 18–19.

Kaplan A., Haenlein M. (2012) The Britney Spears universe: Social media and viral marketing at its best. *Business Horizons, 55*(1), 27–31.

Kaplan A., Haenlein M. (2016) Higher education and the digital revolution: MOOCs, SPOCs, Social Media, and the Cookie Monster. *Business Horizons, 59*(4), 441–450.

Kaplan A., Haenlein M. (2019) Siri, Siri in my hand, who's the fairest in the land? On the interpretations, illustrations, and implications of artificial intelligence. *Business Horizons, 62*(1), 15–25.

Kaplan A., Haenlein M. (2020) Rulers of the world, unite! The challenges and opportunities of artificial intelligence. *Business Horizons, 63*(1), 37–50.

Knight E., Staunton T., Healy M. (2022) University career services' interaction with edtech. In A. Kaplan (ed.), *Digital transformation and disruption of higher education* (pp. 303–315). Cambridge University Press.

Liesaputra V., Ott C. (2022) "Learning analytics enriched by emotions" in A. Kaplan (ed.), *Digital transformation and disruption of higher education* (pp. 361–376). Cambridge University Press.

Malagocka K., Mazurek G., Kaplan A. (2022) Virtual worlds, virtual reality, and augmented reality: Review, synthesis, and research agenda. In Z. Yan (ed.), *The Cambridge handbook of cyber behavior.* Cambridge University Press.

Mazurek G. (2022) 'Real change comes from the outside': COVID-19 as a great opportunity for the revival of business schools and management education. In E. Cornuel (ed.), *Business school leadership and crisis exit planning, Global Deans' Contributions on the Occasion of the 50th Anniversary of the EFMD* (pp. 331–350). Cambridge University Press.

McFarland M. (2016) What happened when a professor built a chatbot to be his teaching assistant. *Washington Post*, May 11.

Murphy V. L., Iniesto F., Scanlon E. (2022) "Higher education's digitalisation: Past, present, and future. In A. Kaplan (ed.), *Digital transformation and disruption of higher education* (pp. 9–21). Cambridge University Press.

Neely, M. P., Tribunella, T., Tang, Z., Hull, C. E. (2008) What influences salary: A study of MIS faculty job offers. *Review of Business Information Systems, 12*(3), 5–20.

Pucciarelli F., Cobo-Benita J. (2022) Artificial intelligence: An adaptive learning methodology. In A. Kaplan (ed.), *Digital transformation and disruption of higher education* (pp. 120–129). Cambridge University Press.

Rubio D., Lastra C., Frey C. B., Colclough C., Jonsson O., de Tena C. L., Menéndez I. (2019) *European tech insights 2020*. IE University.

Seeletso M. K. (2022) "Social exclusion and the digital divide: Digitalisation's dark side" in A. Kaplan (ed.), *Digital transformation and disruption of higher education* (pp. 34–44). Cambridge University Press.

Shcheglova I., Vilkova K., Dremova O. (2022) Online learning: Expectations versus reality. In A. Kaplan (ed.), *Digital transformation and disruption of higher education* (pp. 22–33). Cambridge University Press.

Sporn B. (2022) Strategic Continuity? Or disruption? Adaptive structures of business schools in times of crisis. In E. Cornuel (ed.), *Business school leadership and crisis exit planning. Global Deans' contributions on the occasion of the 50th anniversary of the EFMD* (pp. 197–214). Cambridge University Press.

ThePowerMBA (2022) Frequently asked questions. *ThePowerMBA.com*, available at https://www.thepowermba.com/en/faq.

Vermeulen F. (2005) On rigor and relevance: Fostering dialectic progress in management research. *Academy of Management Journal, 48*, 978–982.

Zawacki-Richter O., Marín V. I., Bond M., Gouverneur F. (2019) Systematic review of research on artificial intelligence applications in higher education: Where are the educators? *International Journal of Educational Technology in Higher Education, 16*, 39.

4 Management Research

Overrated? Or Underexploited?

Not long ago, business schools' approach to research was described as "underperforming" in an article published in the *Financial Times*, where it was claimed that professors increasingly study "abstract, abstruse, and overly academic topics with little resonance beyond the higher education sector" (Jack 2020). A bit earlier, an article in *BizEd* stated that management schools' research models are unsustainable (Glick, Tsui, and Davis 2018). In several articles in the *Harvard Business Review*, one recurrently reads that business school research needs to become more relevant (Eckhardt and Wetherbe 2014; Shapiro and Kirkman 2018), led by the *HBR* landmark article, "How Business Schools Lost Their Way" by Bennis and O'Toole (2005).

Before there are any misunderstandings, many faculty members world-wide – most likely even the majority – would like to see a change in the system. One proof thereof is the recent establishment of the RRBM (Responsible Research in Business and Management) network, which aims at promoting the production and dissemination of managerially and societally relevant management research, with many business schools and accreditation bodies worldwide having joined and actively participating therein. My discussions with colleagues confirm this desire for a new system. And of course many academics already conduct meaningful, responsible, and impactful research. But ultimately, you do what you are incentivized to do, myself included: it's all about motivation and how business school leadership rewards various research outputs.

Since the entry of scientific research production into what were until then vocational schools, business schools have been continuously criticized for this addition to their portfolio of activities. Returning to the history of management schools and tracing how for many of them, especially top-tier institutions, research has slowly but surely become their main preoccupation, explains the regrettable reality of management research. It moreover shows how and why an initially good idea and the sensible purpose of business schools' scientization did not play out as originally intended. Much has indeed gone awry. What are the reasons for this predicament? Is business research overrated? Or underexploited? In post-pandemic times, it appears to make sense for academic institutions to consider research as an important

DOI: 10.4324/9781003343509-4

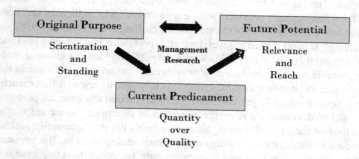

Figure 4.1 Management Research: Purpose > Predicament > Potential

differentiator to incoming, science-weak actors bolstered by the sector's rapid digital transformation. Business schools should position themselves as academic strongholds in contrast to non-academic, teaching-only, edtech startups, and other alternatives developed by big tech giants. Management research is underexploited, not overrated. However, the status quo of scientific research hyper-production must change in order to tap into its full potential. Several remedies and solutions are described, suggested, and vigorously promoted herein.

4.1 Initial Idea and Original Purpose

When looking at the issue of research in business schools, history is a good starting point (Kaplan 2014, 2018). In contrast to the first stand-alone European business schools, the US ones, collegiate in nature, were instantly accused by their non-management counterparts from established academic disciplines of detracting from their universities' academic standing (Engwall and Zamagni 1998). This negative judgment triggered a strong desire to develop academic-level management science in these US schools toward attaining academic standing, a process that aligned with the Wharton School's initial idea: turning business studies from a trade into a rigorous profession. Highly influential pioneering management consultant Frederick W. Taylor advocated for the establishment of a genuine management discipline "resting upon clearly defined laws, rules, and principles, as a foundation" (Taylor 1911, p. 7).

This continuous drive to gain respect within the academia (Khurana 2007) was strongly validated by the Gordon-Howell (1959) Report for the Ford Foundation, which reported dissatisfaction with management education not being founded upon scientific research. Badly functioning business education was claimed to be detrimental to the American way of life, the US economy, and even democracy. Subsequently, the US government transferred huge financial means to management schools with the aim of scientizing business studies. The biggest beneficiaries thereof were the top US schools, several of them having been provided with, e.g., a "mere" $35 million by the Ford Foundation over the 1960s (Schlossmann, Sedlak, and Wechsler 1998). In exchange, schools agreed to several reforms: professors had to hold a PhD and were to publish (lots of) scientific works. As publishing led to additional funding, a professor's scientific output was directly linked to an increase in the respective institution's budget, giving much weight to research (over teaching). Several scientific journals "saw the light" around this time, all pursuing the aim of developing a scientific management discipline. So we see that at the time of their establishment, business schools did not necessarily seek to produce research; they had little or no intrinsic reason to do so. But pressure from other disciplines, as well as from the state, prompted them to pursue scientization. Perhaps they also felt themselves inferior to other disciplines, and sought to remedy that. This might help to explain the current situation, with business schools investing significant resources into relatively little impactful research outcome.

With the notable exception of management education in Germany, with Humboldt's tradition of education through science blurring the line between scientific and educational activities, most of Europe's business schools rejected for quite some time what was considered theory-intensive business education. But the end of World War II also meant an Americanization of European management schools (Kaplan 2014): European countries' economies were shattered, and the US model of management education quickly became an important "weapon of social change" (Leavitt 1957, p. 155). A me-too phenomenon took hold among Europe's institutions as they sought to imitate the more reputed US business schools. While some countries, e.g., France, initially were more resistant thereto, in others, such as Spain and the UK, Americanization was more notable (Engwall and Zamagni 1998). Again, (European) business schools did not want to genuinely produce research, but felt pressured to do so. One could say that business schools were under the impression that to exist, they needed to publish in the top – mostly US-based – academic journals. The sheer number of publications overtook their quality and actual content. The initial idea of introducing management research into business schools was thus only partly achieved: while scientization took place, it did not result in high standing among academic disciplines. The relevance of management research simply did not (yet) exist.

Moreover, to prove that management is a science, researchers began overstressing mathematics and economics in their work, the subjects most similar to the hard sciences. In my discipline, marketing, e.g., one of the top-ranked A+ journals, *Marketing Science*, more or less (rather more than less) consists of mathematical formulas. To publish an article therein, you need some dead-serious math skills. While this in itself is not problematic, the issue is that to translate a marketing phenomenon into a formula, it will have to be based on overly simplified or even knowingly wrong assumptions, as results being consistent with reality and predictive accuracy outweighs making accurate assumptions. Nonetheless, many – especially top-tier – schools are prone to weighing research over teaching in their tenure or promotion requirements, often uniquely depending on a professor's publication record, and not on his or her pedagogical skills. Some top business schools have even built their entire faculty recruiting strategy on hiring only applicants with PhDs in non-management disciplines such as mathematics, econometrics, or psychology (obviously with a strong background in statistics). Apparently these skills improve one's chances of being published in A+ journals more than does solid experience in management studies. We would do well to reflect upon this irony.

As we're in history mode, I'll talk about my own research and its evolution over time. My first A+ journal article (Haenlein, Kaplan, and Schoder 2006) – the one that we consider to have garnered my first job as a professor – took hard work, sweat, and tears (of sadness when rejection mails dropped into our inboxes, as well as tears of joy when we received notice of acceptance). In contrast, the paper for which I am known in the field is a strongly managerial, non-scientific article published in *Business Horizons*, conceptually defining and classifying social media while providing abundant examples from the business world (Kaplan and Haenlein 2010). That first paper took hundreds of hours to produce, while the managerial piece took around three weeks of thinking and writing, and was accepted over a weekend. I am still extremely grateful for the eagerness of *BH* Editor-in-chief Catherine Dalton to publish this timely paper in a record time frame. While that short time frame is an exception, it is an example of how publishing can go. Moreover, the first paper is cited fewer than 200 times in Google Scholar (which is already relatively high with a visible paper to be considered as such, starting at around 30 citations, as a rule of thumb), while the *BH* paper has accrued nearly 30,000 citations. With time and reputation, publishing did get easier, not because of my improved research skills (over time rather decreasing with an increasing workload in higher education administration), or because I wrote more meaningful papers, but rather due to being better known in the field, learning how the game of publishing is played, and being invited to write friendly peer-reviewed articles.

As aforementioned, business schools' preoccupation with research finally led to the creation of the RRBM network in 2015, supported by many management schools and international accreditors worldwide. Its aim is to promote management research that is useful to society, i.e., to develop responsible research (Haenlein et al. 2022; Kohli and Haenlein 2021; Tsui 2013), defined as the production of valuable knowledge, reached with reasonably rigorous methodology, substantially improving the world of business and society at large. As management researchers, our knowledge should benefit businesses, yet ultimately must benefit society, and aim at a sustainable planet. Methodology and applied methods should not be overly and unnecessarily complex, potentially strongly limiting a study's relevance and reach. That's as far as I'll venture into the rigor-vs.-relevance debate. The RRBM network, for its part, aspires by 2030, for business schools to be "widely admired for their contributions to societal wellbeing," with their "timely and cutting-edge" research production resulting in "well-grounded knowledge on pressing problems" (RRBM Network 2022). As such, RRBM, seeks to tackle the second, qualitative, aspect of business schools' quest for standing among the academic disciplines. There have already been several initiatives and appeals for responsible management research in the past and it remains to be seen how efficient this network will be, or if it simply follows the familiar trend of acknowledging a problem without any real change happening.

4.2   Regrettable Reality and Current Predicament

The pursuit of academic acceptance has led to a schism between the needs of business schools for training their students to meet real business challenges, and academia's desire for peer-reviewed, often disconnected-from-reality, increasingly complicated theory building (Dostabler and Tomberlin 2013; Schmalensee 2006). Management research is published in a limited number of specialized journals, rather inaccessible to layfolk, with low readership and impact (Hambrick 1994; Porter and McKibbin 1988). Researchers are incentivized to publish fast and in quantity, and they rarely discuss with practitioners what research questions would interest the professional world. Rather, they research topics about which data is readily available, with the result that management research questions are rarely interesting. The most impactful research – exceptions aside – is the fruit of several years of work, investigation, and longitudinal studies. Taking time to produce results does, however, not match the expectations of management academics and their institutions to get a maximum of articles published in prestigious journals.

Salary increases and promotions of management school professors are mainly based on their volume of peer-reviewed articles in leading scientific journals (Adler and Harzing 2009; Pfeffer 2007; Vermeulen 2005). Some institutions do not even look at teaching quality or administration or leadership skills. For them, it's all about research, with the result that some business schools hire professors purely based on their research output; they are expected to publish, not teach, which in more cases than not leads to resentment by their (teaching) colleagues. An academic career thus comes to depend upon a number of published papers, not on quality of teaching. One might wonder why the jealousy: the higher prestige of researchers (in contrast to superb pedagogues) is so strongly internalized that even "star" instructors who love teaching and are admired by their students, can feel inferior to "research faculty."

Managers rarely read academic journals in order to be on top of the latest research and academic insights (Davis, McKiernan, and Tsui 2022; Rynes, Bartunek, and Daft 2001). Researchers write for their peers, with their results largely unknown to the corporate world. This situation leads to managers continuing to believe and work with (outdated) concepts and theories learned decades ago (Rynes, Brown, Colbert, and Hansen 2002), perhaps somewhat updated by blogs, articles, or Wikipedia entries (Kaplan and Haenlein 2014). Even worse, if a manager learned a since-disproved theory during her studies, in contrast to other academic disciplines, it can lead to a self-fulfilling prophecy. For example, students who are taught that managers usually maximize shareholder value only without considering other stakeholders, will most likely behave accordingly, the least reason being feeling less guilty for behaving thusly, as "they learned it in business school." In contrast, physics students being taught that gravity doesn't exist does not alter reality: a laptop thrown out of a window will still fall to the ground.

When considering the cost of doing research at business schools, this status quo is all the more surprising. AASCB-accredited schools annually spend around $4 billion dollars on research (Glick, Tsui, and Davis 2018), budgets which could in many cases be better spent on other activities. Even more astonishing is that many research faculty feel undercompensated for their research activity, while business schools' administrations feel that compensation levels for such faculty are untenable. Moreover, students, corporations, and media outlets appear not to grasp the value of research produced at business schools, with deans often in trouble and gasping when asked to explain the purpose of management research to media outlets or other stakeholders in general, and more so when asked about research production at their own institution in particular. Just do the test: next time you meet a business school dean, ask her about the number of A+ journal publications her professors produced in the previous year. Then ask her if she can tell you some of an article's content, or even its managerial relevance a bit more in detail.

One argument often brought forward is that research's *raison d'être* at business schools is its being integrated into the teaching. Yet the reality is that to attract the best research-active professors, institutions roll out the red carpet, and sweeten the deal by promising a very limited teaching load: it's not uncommon for top researchers at leading institutions to teach one core course per year, leaving almost no room for incorporating their rather focused, dare I say even narrow, research and academic expertise into their teaching. Moreover, many professors actually teach very different topics than what they research (Lee and Quddus 2008). This might actually be gratifying to students, who often complain about too-theoretical courses without insights from the "real" world, and who prefer talks and courses taught by professionals, want to hear CEOs tell about their experiences, and who often regret the non-applicability of their coursework to their internships or entry-level jobs. In this vein, students' reluctance to relate to and aversion to research often lead professors (even strong researchers) not to include research at all (or at least not make it evident) in their courses.

One might ask why deans worldwide do not simply tackle the status quo, which is not only strongly criticized, but a majority of the management research community deplores it. Accreditations and rankings are repeatedly cited in response to the question of why there is this push for quantity in publications. While it is true to a certain extent that accreditors look at research output, in many cases, they only look for a minimum of research per faculty member, and more importantly, an institution's coherent research strategy (independent of the number of articles published in A+ journals). Moreover, in most cases, rankings do not overstress research. One of the most important rankings, at least for European business schools, that of the *Financial Times*, incorporates research parameters into their MBA and Executive MBA league tables only, and even then counting for a mere 10% of the total result.

Often I surmise that the real reason for deans' desire for a high number of A+ articles published at their institutions is twofold: firstly, to become Dean of a major business school, they themselves most likely published intensively in those outlets, and are justifiably proud of their achievements and many hours invested therein. Thus they replicate what they are familiar with and what made their careers, most likely even leading to their Dean positions. Secondly, there is peer pressure among deans worldwide, many of whom wish to boast of their faculty's strength in research, and brag about the number of top journal publications their professors produced this year. They are justifiably proud of their faculty's achievements, and talking about them in numbers is much easier than doing so in qualitative terms. This is no different than deans talking how many thousands of students they oversee, versus being responsible for only a couple of hundred enrollees at an institution, but speaking highly of their detailed skillsets and competencies. As such, in the job market for business school deans, the interview question not unfrequently is rather "How many students have you been accountable for in your purview?" versus "What achievements and pedagogical improvements have you implemented during your term?" or "What measures did you implement to increase the production of A+ journal papers?" versus "How do you incentivize your faculty to do responsible, meaningful, and relevant research?" Yes, in our case…size matters!

4.3   Vital Vision and Future Potential

Research is firstly important, secondly underexploited… and thirdly a way to differentiate business schools from non-academic, non-research-producing alternative education providers (Kaplan 2022, Kaplan 2021a,b). Two issues need remedying to tap into management research's full potential: relevance and reach (Pucciarelli and Kaplan 2016, 2017, 2019). Both should be part of incentive systems encouraging professors to publish purposeful and highly visible research. Instead of counting the sheer number of professors' A+ publications, institutions should look at the number of downloads and citations of their scientific work, as well as their mentions in newspapers, websites, and social media (Kaplan 2012, Kaplan and Haenlein 2010) or dedicated research platforms such as ResearchGate or academia.edu.

In addition, publications' quality and content must be assessed across all outlets: articles, books, chapters, and further (research) formats. Often the most visible works to those outside academia are monographs or highly managerial (press) articles, which in many cases are freely accessible online. Professors underperforming in publishing articles might be high performers in writing books that might attain high promotional value and visibility not only in academia, but also beyond. Faculty recruiters also should value a candidate's coherence within their research portfolio, which significantly increases one's visibility and reputation within the research community or broader public. Such an evaluation can only be done on a case-by-case basis, and requires effort and resources, which given the high cost of research, should not be a barrier. Take a look at the San Francisco Declaration on Research Assessment (DORA), alerting us to misuses and abuses of simple publication metrics for individual research assessment, particularly for hiring and promotion, and providing advice for the entire research ecosystem such as journals, accreditation and funding bodies, institutions, and researchers themselves. A wholistic evaluation of a professor without necessarily having to follow precise parameters might be preferable. While such a change may appear to render tenure less certain or more arbitrary, it is up to the institution to create an atmosphere of trust, fairness, and psychological well-being to enable a more comprehensive approach to tenure or promotion decisions to be acceptable.

Academics will not only have to be incentivized, but also trained in producing relevant research, as they are increasingly unfamiliar with what this means. Often, professors begin their PhDs directly out of Master's programs, having never seen a company from the inside except for a couple of internships. As aforementioned, in some business schools, many professors have not even studied management, but rather mathematics, psychology, or economics: skills more helpful and likely to lead to A+ publication. So how should they know what is relevant to companies? Well, a business school should provide opportunities for them to learn about it: business schools should encourage their professors to engage with practitioners regularly as part of their job responsibilities (Hambrick 1994; Rynes, Bartunek, and Daft 2001). This could be done by organizing gatherings and brainstorming sessions between alumni, company representatives, and faculty. One could also imagine media training with specialized journalists for professors to grasp what might draw attention from both the business media landscape and the broader public. Of course we can't compel professors to participate in such events, as they might feel it to be an infringement on their academic freedom, which must be respected. But we can certainly offer the opportunity.

Yet, it is not only up to the individual professor to do what it takes to produce high-visibility research. Especially when it comes to research dissemination, institutions are called to duty. While research provides a fantastic opportunity for schools' branding, communication teams are often understaffed and/or lack the necessary competencies for research dissemination. Given the high cost of research in the first place, this is all the more regrettable. A one-page advertisement in *The Economist*, e.g., can cost over $100,000. An article about a professor's research in *The Economist* would be free. Moreover, such an article in marketing terms is considered PR, which is far more credible than paid-for advertising.

Some schools ask their faculty to post a blog entry based on their research every time they are published in a scientific journal, to augment the article's reach and visibility. While this appears to be a good idea, remember that professors are not media experts; they can't be assumed to know how to write an optimal blog post. Therefore, why not provide them with a precise template indicating total length, paragraph length, (short) title length, and number of (short) subheadings, as well as including a minimum number of search-friendly keywords at the beginning of the text best connecting it to a current event or trend. Such a blog post published on the school's website can subsequently lead to the named research getting published in an independent outlet. Infographics on social media, videos, and podcasts are other ways that information is widely consumed by the public. Yet another way to attract the attention of the media to one's research is to organize events on current and timely topics, featuring practitioners, politicians, and known personalities, where professors could give objective research insights into political policy, approaches, and management styles of C-level executives or just famous people and their opinions. This is a way to show the value of scientific research and differentiate it from spin and opinions.

Open access should be enabled systematically, i.e., to make scientific articles available to all, without having to subscribe to a given platform. Business schools have to pay a fee to the journal and publisher to allow their faculty and students access thereto. While these fees seem quite high, they're negligible compared to the overall cost of research. Remember: a scientific article costs around $400,000 (Byrne 2014). Yet I often hear that business schools do not finance open access that costs $1,000–$2,500, as it is considered too costly. But not going all the way – stopping at 95% – reduces an article's impact and visibility significantly, rendering the initial 95% a lot less valuable, if you think about it.

Finally, it would be extremely helpful if rankings changed their criteria to metrics, which clearly would incentivize research's quality and managerial and societal relevance (versus quantity). Of course this is easier said than done, and currently, several league tables are working on changing their evaluation parameters, but the question of metrics often sets limitations. Regardless, even

Responsible Research
is the production of valuable knowledge, arrived at via reasonably rigorous methodology, which substantially improves the world of business and society at large.

Relevance	Reach
• Incentivize quality over quantity of research production. • Train faculty on what it means to do relevant, responsible research. • Encourage regular, voluntary meetings with practitioners. • Establish journalists<>faculty contacts to find out what media is interested in. • Convince rankings and accreditors to value relevance, not mass production.	• Assess a faculty member's research production on their visibility. • Broaden potential publication outlets beyond A+ journals to a maximum. • Ensure that communication teams have the means to disseminate research. • Provide professors with media training and templates. • Generalize the financing of publications' open access.

Only business schools' leadership can bring real, authentic change to the system.

Figure 4.2 Responsible Research: Relevance and Reach

if they come up with better indicators, one thing needs to be clear: metrics can in most cases be "played" and contoured. Business schools shooting for high rankings in league tables will always find a way to optimize the criteria regardless of actual research relevance and reach. Ultimately, it must be the business schools themselves that want to change the system toward producing more impactful and responsible research. It is about the dean and a business school's administration developing a vital vision and implementation plan for relevant, responsible, and highly visible research production.

References

Adler N. J., Harzing A. W. (2009) When knowledge wins: Transcending the sense and nonsense in academic rankings, *Academy of Management Learning & Education*, 8, 72–95.

Bennis W., O'Toole J. (2005) How business schools lost their way. *Harvard Business Review*, *83*(5), 96–104.

Byrne J. A. (2014) Cost of an Academic Article: $400K. *Poets & Quants*, July 16, available online at https://poetsandquants.com/2014/07/16/the-shockingly-high-cost-of-an-academic-article-400k/.

Davis G. F., McKiernan P., Tsui A. S. (2022) Multi- and interdisciplinary research in a world of crisis: A responsible research solution. In E. Cornuel (ed.), *Business School Leadership and Crisis Exit Planning, Global Deans' Contributions on the Occasion of the 50th Anniversary of the EFMD* (pp. 71–90). Cambridge University Press.

Dostaler I., Tomberlin T. J. (2013) The great divide between business school research and business practice. *Canadian Journal of Higher Education*, *43*(1), 115–128.

Eckardt J., Wetherbe J. C. (2014) Making business school research more relevant. *Harvard Business Review*, December 24.

Engwall L., Zamagni, V. (1998). *Management education in historical perspective.* Manchester University Press.

Glick W., Tsui A., Davis G. (2018) The moral dilemma to business research. *AACSB BizEd*, May 2, 32–37.

Gordon R. A., Howell J. E. (1959) *Higher education for business.* Columbia University Press.

Haenlein M., Kaplan A., Schoder D. (2006) Valuing the real option of abandoning unprofitable customers when calculating customer lifetime value. *Journal of Marketing, 70*(3), 5–20.

Haenlein M., Bitner M. J., Kohli A. K., Lemon K. N., Reibstein D. J. (2022) Responsible research in marketing. *Journal of the Academy of Marketing Science, 50*(1), 8–12.

Hambrick D. C. (1994) What if the Academy actually mattered? *Academy of Management Review, 19*: 11–18.

Jack A. (2020) Academic focus limits business schools' contribution to society. *Financial Times*, February 24.

Kaplan A. (2012) If you love something, let it go mobile: Mobile marketing and mobile social media 4×4. *Business Horizons, 55*(2), 129–139.

Kaplan A. (2014) European Management and European Business Schools: Insights from the history of business schools. *European Management Journal, 32*(4), 529–534.

Kaplan A. (2018) "A School is a Building that Has 4 Walls – with Tomorrow Inside": Toward the reinvention of the business school. *Business Horizons, 61*(4), 599–608.

Kaplan A. (2021a) Higher education at the crossroads of disruption: The university of the 21st century. In *Great debates in higher education*. Emerald Publishing.

Kaplan A. (2021b) *Professionals need to keep their skills fresh. Will they turn to higher ed?* Harvard Business Publishing, September 17, 2021, available online at https://www.hbsp.harvard.edu/inspiring-minds/professionals-need-to-keep-their-skills-fresh-will-they-turn-to-higher-ed/?ab=top_nav.

Kaplan A. (2022) *Digital transformation and disruption of higher education.* Cambridge University Press.

Kaplan A., Haenlein M. (2010) Users of the world, unite! The challenges and opportunities of social media. *Business Horizons, 53*(1), 59–68.

Kaplan A., Haenlein M. (2014) Collaborative projects (social media application): About Wikipedia, the free encyclopedia. *Business Horizons, 57*(5), 617–626.

Khurana R. (2007) *From higher aims to hired hands: The social transformation of American business schools and the unfulfilled promise of management as a profession.* Princeton University Press.

Kohli A. K., Haenlein M. (2021) Factors affecting the study of important marketing issues: Implications and recommendations. *International Journal of Research in Marketing, 38*(1), 1–11.

Leavitt H. J. (1957) On the export of American management education. *Journal of Business, 30*, 153–161.

Lee B. B., Quddus M. (2008) AACSB standards and accounting faculty's intellectual contributions. *Journal of Education for Business, 83*(3) 173–180.

Pfeffer J. (2007) A modest proposal: How might we change the process and product of managerial research? *Academy of Management Journal, 50*, 1334–1345.

Porter L. W., McKibbin L. E. (1988) *Management education and development: Drift? Or thrust into the 21ˢᵗ century?* McGraw Hill.

Pucciarelli F., Kaplan A. (2016) Competition and strategy in higher education: Managing complexity and uncertainty. *Business Horizons, 59*(3), 311–320.

Pucciarelli F., Kaplan A. (2017) Le Università Europee oggi: Sfide e nuove strategie. *Economia & Management*, gennaio/febbraio, *1*, 85–95.

Pucciarelli F., Kaplan A. (2019) Competition in higher education. In B. Nguyen, T. C. Melewar, J. Hemsley-Brown (eds.) *Strategic brand management in higher education*. Routledge.

RRBM Network (2022) Vision 2030: Responsible research in business & management network. https://www.rrbm.network/position-paper/vision-2030/.

Rynes S. L., Bartunek J. M., Daft R. L. (2001) Across the great divide: Knowledge creation and transfer between practitioners and academics. *Academy of Management Journal, 44*(2), 340–355.

Rynes S. L., Brown K. G., Colbert A. E., Hansen R. A. (2002) Seven common misconceptions about human resource practices: Research findings versus practitioner beliefs. *Academy of Management Executive, 16*(3), 92–103.

Schlossman S., Sedlack M., Wechsler H. (1998) The Ford Foundation and the revolution in business education. In R. R. Locke (ed.), *Management education* (pp. 3–20). Ashgate.

Schmalensee R. (2006) Where's the "B" in b-schools? *Business Week, 118*, November 27.

Shapiro D. L., Kirkman B. (2018) It's time to make business school research more relevant. *Harvard Business Review*, July 19.

Taylor F. W. (1911) *The principles of scientific management*. Harper Bros.

Tsui A. S. (2013) The spirit of science and socially responsible scholarship. *Management and Organization Review, 9*(3), 375–394.

Vermeulen F. (2005) On rigor and relevance: Fostering dialectic progress in management research. *Academy of Management Journal, 48*, 978–982.

5 Teaching Management
Tough Mission?

Whether management skills are teachable has been discussed and dissected since business schools' inception more than 200 years ago. The belief that commerce and management could only be learned on the job – not in the classroom – was not uncommon. ESCP, the world's pioneer in business education, was originally funded by a group of private businessmen in 1819. Not until 1869 did the Paris Chamber of Commerce acquire the school and reverse its decision not to finance the school at its establishment, with the Chamber refusing any institutionalization of educating managers and entrepreneurs from a theoretical and school-like orientation (Lemercier 2003). Two centuries later, many non-believers in theoretical management education still exist. Moreover, business students often have the impression (and complain thereabout) of not learning much of importance vis-à-vis their internship or future job. In many cases, they prefer listening to industry experts, gaining experience doing internships, and learning to manage and lead in their extracurricular pursuits.

Obviously, we as management academics believe that management is teachable. Actually, some who share that belief blame business schools (even from within) for being responsible for many global problems due to what is taught in finance, logistics, marketing, and strategy classes worldwide. Thus we hear University of Leicester Professor Martin Parker's (2018) demand to "Shut Down the Business School," and asking in his book titled *What's Wrong with Management Education?* Students were purportedly once taught that management means maximizing their returns at the expense of others. Not only is this no longer the case (if it ever was), but since the 2008 financial crisis and associated critique of business schools, the latter made it a priority to scrutinize syllabi and curricula and to include and strengthen the dimensions of corporate social responsibility, business ethics, diversity, and sustainability (Kaplan 2021 c,d; Pucciarelli and Kaplan 2019, 2021). Even before 2008, many researchers contended that business schools are teaching the wrong subjects in the wrong way (e.g., Datar, Garvin, and Cullen 2010; Ghoshal 2005; Khurana and Spender 2012; Locke and Spender 2011; Mintzberg 2004).

Non-traditional educational providers, increasingly crowding the management education market, seemingly deliver the same (academic) content as

DOI: 10.4324/9781003343509-5

business schools for a fraction of the cost and with much shorter program durations. How should established institutions remain competitive and teach business in such a threatening and ever-tougher landscape? To justify longer program length and higher tuition, business schools need to provide students with experiences in an integrative manner across various activities such as course work, internships, study abroad, and supporting participation in extra-curriculars and volunteering. Longer program duration should be marketed as an advantage, with students gaining skills and competencies that they would not be able to in brief online training such as Google's Career Certificates. While research output as well provides a potential for differentiation in an increasingly fierce competitive landscape, it cannot be stand-alone, but rather must be integrated with practice and teaching, explicitly and extensively. Finally, an academic management program should span a multitude of disciplines within and outside the business domain. Interdisciplinarity fosters adaptability, flexibility, and autonomous learning – capabilities necessary to thrive in employment markets characterized by job definitions that change at the speed of mobile device updates.

5.1   Time and Experience

Big tech giant Google's Career Certificates provides participants with six months of online courses and promises successful graduates job interviews that are usually granted to four-year Bachelor's graduates. Comparing six months and fees of a few hundred dollars with four years of studying with costs likely around €100,000 indicates the seriousness of the new competitive landscape that business schools are navigating (Boatman and Borowiec 2022; Schlegelmilch 2020). Studies show that grades and academic performance are not good predictors of actual success as a manager and job performance. Analyzing 1,000 Harvard Business School graduates, Gordon Marshall (1964, p. 21) confirmed, "Academic success and business achievement have relatively little association with each other." Might this be a point in favor of shorter and far less costly studies?

To justify longer program duration and higher tuition, business schools must add value beyond teaching content; they must provide experiences toward graduating skilled, responsible, and well-rounded future business leaders. Business schools must ensure that students – whether undergraduate or graduate – are more apt to succeed in business than those with a short and low-cost certificate in their pocket. They need to package various activities and ensure that four years of studies yield a plethora of experiences that students could not get within six or fewer months. This means bundling activities, i.e., course work, internships, study abroad, student life, and volunteering and/or mentoring. Business schools need to make sure that these domains are interlinked and play into one another, providing a wholistic experience. While business schools already do so, they must ramp up this effort substantially. Only thusly will high tuitions and long durations be justifiable.

Business schools furthermore need to strengthen their students' flexibility, contextual adaptability, and general know-how (Kaplan 2018). In an environment where job requirements quickly change and associated knowledge outdates likewise, students must be prepared to constantly adjust to new contexts and situations (Fragueiro 2022). Accordingly, Datar, Garvin, and Cullen (2010) downplayed the importance of cognitive knowledge and called for more attention to the "doing and being" aspects of professionalism. Switching from the traditional transmission of knowledge to training for adaptability and a do-it-yourself approach will help students get into the habit of and engage in lifelong and continuous learning. Over the next decade, more than a billion jobs worldwide will be transformed by advances in artificial intelligence, robotics, and digitization (Haenlein, Huang, and Kaplan 2022; Kaplan 2020; Kaplan and Haenlein 2019, 2020). Such a transformation in job markets will demand acquiring new competencies, skills, and knowledge throughout one's professional life as lifelong learning, reskilling, and upskilling have become undisputed components of being employed (Kaplan 2022a).

A business school must be about personal growth via significant experiences. Research testifies that students achieve substantial insights and learn new skills and competencies by studying abroad and doing internships. While this is definitely the case, it is not enough. Students need to feel a real value added from such experiences. After all, what more do business schools currently do in terms of a student's semester abroad aside from connecting them with the partner institution? One could ask the same question regarding internships. Suppose students have the impression that they did the brunt of organizing such a venture on their own, or worse, some third-party entity is responsible for their experience. How can business schools justify longer program durations or higher tuition? In the same time frame as a semester abroad or a summer internship, a student could enroll in Google's Career Certificates, find an internship on his or her own, and/or enroll in a summer program in a country that he or she wants to discover. Accordingly, business schools need to design experiences and organize them in such a way as to deliver true value to their students.

Take for example the career service, a pillar of business schools' student services (Arnold 2018). With the help of a dedicated career consultant, students should be empowered to identify their ideal first job to fulfill them professionally. In career counseling, internship experiences should be discussed and analyzed to help the student find the right professional path. Career counseling sessions should go beyond strictly finding the student employment, but rather include reflections on which partner university might make sense for gaining international experience that would further the student's professional aspirations; which elective courses would be particularly interesting and useful theretoward; and which alumni might be able to help this student on her journey to fulfilling employment. Such a wholistic approach would be considered to add high value to the student's business school enrollment.

Yet reality shows that we're far away from such service and management of the student experience. In many cases, career services are little more than general, non-personalized CV and interview training. Moreover, business schools have begun outsourcing some career services to edtech startups such as JobTeaser or Jobs2Careers. Alumni traditionally have been grateful to their alma mater having helped them find their first job. If career services are now delivered by edtech platforms, to whom will alumni be grateful? I'm not saying that outsourcing is to be avoided. But I am saying that management schools' career service teams must refind their added value in a landscape littered by career platforms and LinkedIn. To do so, they need to be strongly staffed with highly competent, service-oriented personnel.

The most salient experiences while studying are often making friends and building lifelong networks. In many if not most cases, such friendships are forged outside the classroom, in a dedicated social setting. Alternative educational providers mostly operate online and thereby provide far fewer opportunities for social contacts to form. This should prompt business schools to actively foster such face-to-face socializing opportunities, and facilitate such by organizing special events, field trips, and the like. They also should actively support extracurriculars, by providing them with useful expertise, integrating them into a wholistic package of student experiences. For example, the administration could enable a faculty member who specializes in sustainability to coach a student society whose objective it is to render society more eco-responsible; and the management team of each student society could be offered a particular training course on leadership to strengthen and add value to their experience in leading their society.

This is all to say that a business school must act as an experience booster and a hub, bringing together and amplifying the various experiences in which its students engage. Students need to get the most out of these experiences with the help of their business school – much more than if they'd engaged in an internship, study abroad, or student club leadership without such support and experience enhancement. Such an approach to the organization and augmentation of student experience will set business schools apart from short certification courses offered by edtech and big tech.

5.2   Science and Practice

Can management be taught via theory, or only by learning-by-doing? Is management a science that one learns as one learns math or physics? Or is it practical skills such as that of a dressmaker or a locksmith? According to Herbert Simon (1967), it is both: the one permanently confronting the other, resulting in the convergence of both. To achieve this, professors must profoundly comprehend current managers' and entrepreneurs' challenges, and integrate these into their courses. Moreover, they need to focus their research on precisely these challenges, generating science able to remedy or alleviate managerial problems. Curriculum and syllabus design should undergo a reality check by practitioners and industry experts. Combining science with practice would subsequently teach business students ready-to-apply, business-relevant knowledge. As early as over half a century ago, Simon (1967) predicted that most management schools would fail thereat, insisting that a business school should resemble neither a physics department nor a trade school. The combining of applied problem-solving and scientific knowledge confers business schools their own third place and purpose, apart from the former two.

How should this work? We know that students love practitioners coming to the classroom and talking about their on-the-job experience. We also know that students point to coursework as not being relevant to their future employment. While theories and concepts play a minor role for them, this does not mean that science should not be brought into the classroom, scholars increasingly reducing this kind of content in favor of hands-on, practical examples notwithstanding. Yet the truth is that to differentiate business schools from edtech and big tech players, whose instructors are often high-level practitioners, the integration of science into business school curricula should be strengthened, and courses made more academic. Currently, students are often overstrained when exposed to scientific research and papers in the classroom. To understand (relevant) research and benefit therefrom, students need to be trained in research methodology and reading and comprehending scientific articles. This demands a lot of groundwork, including but not limited to dedicated courses in scientific research. It therefore makes sense to confront and combine science and practice as soon as students can truly understand the scientific method.

To be exposed to science regularly is, moreover, of extreme value in an environment wherein a (former) student's knowledge needs to be regularly updated. We're often asked to autonomously acquire new knowledge and skills throughout our careers. Being grounded in the scientific method facilitates the quest for knowledge. It enables us to identify high-quality information and rigorously attained results, and enables us to differentiate them from groundless thoughts and opinions published in non-scientific outlets. We need to remind students often of this. Precisely because they're skeptical of research and science and "consume" this skepticism online, we need to explain why exposure to research and management science is important. Only if they understand why they should try to comprehend relatively complicated methods and methodologies will we reduce their skepticism about the usefulness of incorporating pure research into the curriculum. From a marketing perspective, a message must be repeated a minimum of three times to be remembered. So we need to make students (repeatedly) aware that having professors who are actively participating in the production of knowledge is a big advantage, as they are likely to be methodologically sophisticated and thus advanced in their field, and have a better and more up-to-date overview of how the field evolves and where it is headed.

Theoretical knowledge and real-life practice (as well as their recurrent juxtaposition to each other both in and outside the classroom) are the pillars of truly valuable learning. My experience with ThePower MBA (cf. Chapter 3) showed me the benefits of integrating short videos of approximately five to ten minutes of successful managers and entrepreneurs telling their stories. These professionally led interviews turned theory into practice. Apart from providing students with real-world insights, such videos would have several additional advantages: alumni would feel appreciated, students could get inspired by their predecessors' careers, and professors would be brought into contact with practitioners. A strategic approach to producing such short testimonials and incorporating them into courses would be highly beneficial to a business school's entire community. Outside the classroom, internships are not only essential, but they're highly relevant and provide students with insights into real professional life. However, they should not be stand-alone and disconnected from coursework, as science should not be taught in the classroom without ample opportunity to apply it. On the contrary, in light of business schools' value in bundling activities, the internship experience should be analyzed and evaluated with coaches and professors for students to understand their gained insights and to comprehend from a scientific point of view what happened during their practical experience of the business world. Internship reports asking students to apply learned theory and concepts to their experience are a good way to encourage them reflect on their observations and bring science and practice together. Such a report should be discussed with a jury of professors and practitioners. While this sounds like a huge effort in terms of organization and resources, given that an internship represents a student's investment of several months, it doesn't seem like a lot to ask for a business school to schedule a couple of coaching sessions and a one-hour jury afterwards. This represents added value, thus justifying tuition and time invested.

The same applies to study abroad. Before going abroad, students should be familiarized with cross-cultural theories and concepts, helping them to obtain significantly more value from their time abroad. De Vita and Case (2003) showed that gaining a genuine immersive experience demands far more than simply boarding a plane and showing up. This is corroborated by Doh (2010), who argued that simply sending students abroad is not sufficient. Think about it: is it not strange to send a student to, let's say, Japan without him or her having taken any courses on Japanese culture or language? This is, however, a regular occurrence. Simply advising students to "inform themselves about their destination" is the equivalent of presenting them with a copy of *Lonely Planet*. With today's online possibilities, it would be easy to organize cultural courses for students going abroad, that are adapted to the chosen destination. Beyond this, business schools could organize tandems with one student being a national of the soon-to-be-visited country and the other preparing to travel.

Or, a tandem of a current student connected to an alumnus residing in the locale where the exchange stay is planned. This would not only provide the student with insights into the other culture, but also give them a first local contact in the target location. Moreover, this fosters a vital sense of community that business schools should "make it their business" to forge and develop (Kaplan 2021a, b).

5.3   Disciplinary and Interdisciplinary

While management disciplines need to be taught at business school, this is not enough. Non-management disciplines must also appear in business schools' curricula more extensively than ever before (Kaplan 2021b; Mintzberg 2004). ESCP's initial curricula balanced scientific studies such as mathematics and political economy with more commerce-oriented subjects such as accounting (Iñiguez 2022; Kaplan 2014). Students were also allowed to enroll in courses at the nearby Conservatoire National des Arts et Métiers, which at the time was essentially an engineering school. In Wharton's early days, students spent the first two years studying liberal arts, followed by a year of studying international and mainly American politics and history, with a final year in management courses including accounting, business law, and business practice (Joullé and Spillane 2020). Wharton founder Joseph Wharton (1890) explained that a graduate should be:

> an educated man knowing something more about his business than the ordinary hand-to-mouth practical man, having a wide view of the relations of his business to other lines of business and society as a whole, and above all, an intelligent citizen, with a quickened interest in everything that concerns his country and his time, and an immensely greater desire and ability to use what he may learn and what he may earn in his business for the benefit of his fellow man.

Over the decades, the multidisciplinary approach to teaching management somehow got left by the wayside, and studies increasingly became disciplinary and specialized (Peters, Smith, and Howards 2018). To find solutions to today's challenges, a multi- and interdisciplinary education makes more sense than ever. Responding to Covid-19, for example, demanded health specialists, legal experts, policymakers, and data engineers, as well as those from the corporate world, all of whom had to collaborate and understand their respective experts' languages. They had to work in multidisciplinary teams and present their ideas and solutions to each other. Already the Sapporo Sustainability Declaration (2008, p. 4) of Tokyo's G8 University Summit underscored that it is incumbent upon academia to educate "leaders with the skills to solve regional and local problems from a global and interdisciplinary perspective," as most societal challenges such as digitization, environmental protection, and the refugee crisis all require multi- and interdisciplinary solutions.

Moreover, companies know the advantages of students familiar with more than one discipline. Recruitment statistics show that students with degrees in more than one discipline are more in demand and are offered higher salaries than those who studied only one discipline, even if the latter holds an advanced degree (García-Álvarez, Vázquez-Rodríguez, Quiroga-Carrillo, and Caamaño 2022). That having been said, some disciplines are always in more demand than others, coding and mastering a programming language being one of them, as companies realize that humans increasingly have to work and collaborate with machines (Kaplan 2022a). Therefore a basic knowledge of the language of machines makes sense, just as speaking a bit of French and knowing about French culture helps when doing business in France.

A multidisciplinary approach to teaching and learning management aims not to produce an expert in everything. Neither does it aim to familiarize students with every facet of several disciplines. While this would be wonderful, it is not feasible unless such a program's duration is lengthened. Thus, not being able to go for both breadth and depth, breadth should be prioritized, the objective being for students to acquire general comprehension of and advanced terminology in several disciplines. Doing so will help bridge discussions in multidisciplinary teams and facilitate mutual understanding. Moreover, if need be, students – especially those with grounding in research methodology – will be able to gain further knowledge in a given discipline and master it relatively quickly. Lifelong learning is subsequently facilitated, having set a solid foundation in various disciplines (Kaplan 2021 a,b).

Additionally, a multi- and interdisciplinary approach to management education develops and cultivates students' critical thinking, which is sorely needed and valued in the job market (Davis 1997; Wilson and Thomas 2012). To have insight into several disciplines, their ways of doing things, their methodologies, and approaches, enables one to view a given problem from various angles and potentially leads to a more critical evaluation of a found solution, compared to if problem-solving was engaged in, and backed up by one discipline only. Disciplinary boundaries have been challenged for a long time, as it has become virtually impossible to acquire the totality of a given field's knowledge. This renders it all the more important to critically look at a proposed solution, balance its advantages and drawbacks, and make an informed decision.

From an operational point of view, academia's digitization facilitates a multi- and interdisciplinary approach to teaching management. Simply put, non-management disciplines can now be enrolled in digitally in another department or partner universities. Especially for stand-alone business schools, scheduling was difficult to impossible, to enable students to take one's own institution's courses and enroll in those at other institutions, as commuting times had to be considered. Online courses – asynchronous or synchronous – are not only a huge bypass of this barrier, but they also facilitate the work of multiple program offices worldwide. The online sphere also enables pooling from geographically distant institutions more than ever before. While pre-remote learning, one was limited to the same locale for attending courses from other disciplines, now time zones and wireless availability are the only limits to doing so (Kaplan 2021a,b).

The digital sphere is also useful for enabling interdisciplinarity, which is even harder to organize than a multidisciplinary approach. While multidisciplinarity demands courses (independently taught) in several disciplines, interdisciplinarity requires comparing and contrasting theories and concepts from various disciplines in the same course (Nissani 1995). Therefore, interdisciplinarity often is taught by pairs of professors who teach a course simultaneously, each bringing their expertise to the subject. Tandems, though, mean higher costs and higher demand for resources. To offset these, some course elements could be delivered asynchronously to larger group sizes, thereby saving some funds, which could then be reinvested in the teaching in pairs for other modules of the course. This arrangement would and should lead to quality optimization while keeping budgets stable.

Teaching management is a tough mission, as aforementioned. While it is about education, it is also increasingly about integrating, coordinating, and accompanying experiences. The combination of education and experience, science and practice, prepares students effectively for future employment, and differentiates management schools from edtech and big tech certificates. Constituting a hub that augments, enhances, and connects various courses across disciplines, internships, study abroad, supporting extracurriculars, holding events, and offering superb career services will

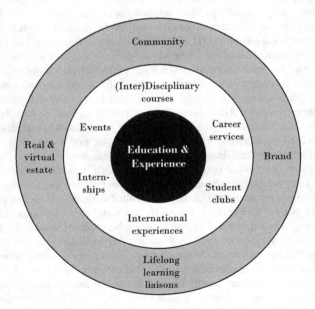

Figure 5.1 The Business School Product: A Student Perspective

set business schools apart and help justify significantly higher tuition and longer program duration. So, on another level, will an institution's branding and community building via its business school transforming into a lifelong learning partner, via its physical plant and real (as well as virtual) estate (cf. Chapters 7 and 8). It all must work in concert to result in well-trained, well-rounded graduates who are prepared for professional life better than they could be by enrolling in alternatives such as Google's Career Certificates or ThePowerMBA.

References

Arnold W. W. (2018) Strengthening college support services to improve student transitioning to careers. *Journal of College Teaching & Learning, 15*(1), 5–25.

Boatman A., Borowiec K. (2022) Degrees of disruption: Alternative educational credentialing. In A. Kaplan (ed.), *Digital transformation and disruption of higher education* (pp. 255–268). Cambridge University Press.

Datar S., Garvin D. A., Cullen P. G. (2010) *Rethinking the MBA: Business education at a crossroads.* Harvard Business Press.

Davis J. R. (1997) *Interdisciplinary courses and team teaching.* American Council on Education/Oryx Press Series on Higher Education.

De Vita G., Case P. (2003) Rethinking the internationalization agenda in UK higher education. *Journal of Further and Higher Education, 27,* 383–398.

Doh J. P. (2010) From the editors: Why aren't business schools more global, and what can management educators do about it? *Academy of Management Learning and Education, 9,* 165–168.

Fragueiro F. J. (2022) "Educating business leaders, but for what kind of world?" in E. Cornuel (ed.), *Business school leadership and crisis exit planning, global deans' contributions on the occasion of the 50th anniversary of the EFMD* (pp. 56–70). Cambridge University Press.

García-Álvarez J., Vázquez-Rodríguez A., Quiroga-Carrillo A., Caamaño D. P. (2022) Transversal competencies for employability in university graduates: A systematic review from the employers' perspective. *Education Sciences, 12*(3), 204.

Ghoshal S. (2005) Bad management theories are destroying good management practices. *Academy of Management Learning & Education, 4*(1), 75–91.

Haenlein M., Huang M.-H., Kaplan A. (2022) Business ethics in the era of artificial intelligence. Special Issue, *Journal of Business Ethics, 178,* 867–869.

Iñiguez S. (2022) From Techne to Paideia: Upgrading business education. In E. Cornuel (ed.), *Business School Leadership and Crisis Exit Planning, Global Deans' Contributions on the Occasion of the 50th Anniversary of the EFMD* (pp. 37–55). Cambridge University Press.

Joullé J. E., Spillane R. (2020) *The philosophical foundations of management thought.* Lexington Books.

Kaplan A. (2014) European management and European business schools: Insights from the history of business schools. *European Management Journal, 32*(4), 529–534.

Kaplan A. (2018) "A School is a Building that Has 4 Walls – with Tomorrow Inside": Toward the reinvention of the business school. *Business Horizons, 61*(4), 599–608.

Kaplan A. (2020) Retailing and the Ethical Challenges and Dilemmas Behind Artificial Intelligence, in P. Eleonora (ed.), *Retail futures: The good, the bad and the ugly of the digital transformation* (pp. 181–191). Emerald Publishing.

Kaplan A. (2021a) Higher education at the crossroads of disruption: The university of the 21st century. In *Great debates in higher education*. Emerald Publishing.

Kaplan A. (2021b) Multi- and interdisciplinarity empowered and entailed by business schools' digitalisation. *efmdglobal.org*, April 29, 2021, available online at https://blog.efmdglobal.org/2021/04/29/multi-and-interdisciplinarity-business-schools-digitalisation/.

Kaplan A. (2021c) *Prepare for student sustainability demands to go through the roof.* THE – Times Higher Education, October 19 2021, available online at https://www.timeshighereducation.com/campus/prepare-student-sustainability-demands-go-through-roof.

Kaplan A. (2021d) The 21st-century university: Societal, sustainable, and responsible research in business and management. *RRBM, www.rrbm.network*, May 7, 2021, available online at https://www.rrbm.network/the-21st-century-university-societal-and-sustainable-andreas-kaplan/.

Kaplan A. (2022a) *Artificial intelligence, business, and civilization: Our fate made in machines*. Routledge.

Kaplan A. (2022b) *Digital transformation and disruption of higher education*. Cambridge University Press.

Kaplan A., Haenlein M. (2019) Siri, Siri in my hand, who's the fairest in the land? On the interpretations, illustrations, and implications of artificial intelligence. *Business Horizons, 62*(1), 15–25.

Kaplan A., Haenlein M. (2020) Rulers of the world, unite! The challenges and opportunities of artificial intelligence. *Business Horizons, 63*(1), 37–50.

Khurana R., Spender J.-C. (2012) Herbert A. Simon on what ails business schools: More than 'A problem in organization design'. *Journal of Management Studies 49*(3), 619–639.

Lemercier C. (2003) La chambre de commerce de Paris, acteur indispensable de la construction des normes économiques (première moitié du xixe siècle). *Genèses, 1*, 50–70.

Locke R. R., Spender J.-C. (2011) *Confronting managerialism: How the business elite and their schools threw our lives out of balance*. Zed Books.

Marshall G. L. (1964) *Predicting executive achievement*. Doctoral Dissertation, Harvard Business School.

Mintzberg H. (2004) *Managers, not MBAs: A hard look at the soft practice of managing and management development*. Berrett-Koehler.

Nissani M. (1995) Fruits, salads, and smoothies: A working definition of interdisciplinarity. *Journal of Educational Thought, 29*(2), 121–128.

Parker M. (2018) *Shut down the business school: What's wrong with management education?* Pluto Press.

Peters K., Smith R. R., Thomas H. (2018) *Rethinking the business models of business schools: A critical review and change agenda for the future*. Emerald Publishing.

Pucciarelli F., Kaplan A. (2019) Competition in higher education. In B. Nguyen, T. C. Melewar, J. Hemsley-Brown (eds.), *Strategic brand management in higher education* (pp. 74–88). Routledge.

Pucciarelli F., Kaplan A. (2021) From narrative to action: Are business schools walking the talk of responsible management education? *efmdglobal.org*, June 28, 2021,

available online at https://blog.efmdglobal.org/2021/06/28/from-narrative-to
-action-are-business-schools-walking-the-talk-of-responsible-management
-education/.

Sapporo Sustainability Declaration (2008) *7. The role of higher education for sustainability.* Tokyo G8 University Summit.

Schlegelmilch B. B. (2020) Why business schools need radical innovations: Drivers and development trajectories. *Journal of Marketing Education, 42*(2) 93–107.

Simon H. A. (1967) The business school, a problem in organizational design. *Journal of Management Studies, 4*(1), 1–16.

Wharton J. (1890) *Is a college education advantageous to a business man?* Address before the Wharton School Association, February 20, University of Philadelphia.

Wilson D. C., Thomas H. (2012) Challenges and criticism: The legitimacy of the business of business schools: What's the future? *Journal of Management Development, 31*(4), 368–376.

6   For What It's Worth
B-School Accreditations and Rankings

To do well in rankings or to be awarded several of the major international accreditation labels (combined in the holy grail of the "Triple Crown" (Jacqmin and Lefebvre 2021)), management schools prove their quality on a number of key performance indicators. For example, to be considered by several accreditation bodies, business schools must prove that half of all courses are taught by permanently employed professors, publishing a minimum quantity of research (itself quantified by certain criteria). This indicator alone influences recruiting decisions of new faculty at business schools worldwide, with more weight recurrently put on research output and less on pedagogy, the latter not rarely being treated as an afterthought (Kaplan 2018).

Business schools' leadership teams spend a lot of time thinking about how to improve ranking positions or how to obtain or keep one of the prestigious accreditation labels. In most cases, the entire institution is mobilized to meet the various parameters in one way or another. Getting accredited and ranked translates into pride for the entire community around a business school, and helps to strengthen and increase brand equity. Losing an accreditation or falling in rankings quickly turns into a PR nightmare, leads to great concern among a business school's stakeholders, and on more than one occasion has led to deans resigning.

Holders of prestigious accreditations such as the AACSB, AMBA, and EFMD's EQUIS, or institutions lucky enough to be highly ranked by the *Financial Times* or *The Economist* are strongly inclined to support these rankings, whereas business schools in the opposite situation are likely to criticize them. Yet even in institutions that are highly ranked, voices can be heard expressing negative opinions of rankings, if only behind closed doors. What is an accreditation's value, and does it make a real difference in a business school's existence and functioning? What are the potential negative consequences of pursuing and obtaining accreditation? What is the rationale and intention of rankings, and what is a ranking position in a certain league table worth? Do certain positions up or down a ranking matter? Accreditations and rankings have been almost the only quality signals that schools could transmit to the market of potential students and executive education participants thus far. Yet digitization increasingly provides business schools with a series of

DOI: 10.4324/9781003343509-6

additional means and internal options at their disposal, potentially decreasing the necessity for third-party warranting. Whatever the case, while labels and rankings certainly represent valuable marketing opportunities, business schools should use them above all to improve, not simply to impress.

6.1   Accreditations Analyzed

Accreditation and reaccreditation processes can be stressful periods in a dean's life, as well as for the entire institution. In particular, initial accreditation can take several years. To get (re)accredited, most accreditors have similar processes in place: a preliminary survey assessing the school; a report written by the school based on an accreditor's specific standards and questions; a site visit by a peer-review team issuing a report with several recommendations; and finally, the decision of the accreditor whether or not to grant the label to the institution and under what conditions. To give one example, let's look at the AACSB's Assurance of Learning (AoL) standards, explained as the process (to be put) in place for demonstrating that students achieve learning expectations for the programs in which they're enrolled. The AoL is issued at the program level, and measures whether graduates master specific competencies (practical, professional, and transferable skills) defined by their alma mater. This means that for each program, you need to identify clear learning goals, i.e., what you want your graduating students to have learned; and show (that is, proof and document) how each course contributes to reaching those goals. Such a process can become a bureaucratic nightmare if not done correctly. Imagine a school with 30 different programs, each consisting of around 25 courses, each with distinct learning goals: you're soon facing thousands of individual indicators to assess.

Accreditation is not equal to accreditation; many international and national accreditations exist. Focusing on the major international business school accreditation bodies, we'll mention three of them: the US accreditation system AACSB and the European EQUIS label provided by the EFMD, both accrediting the entire school; and the UK-based AMBA, accrediting specifically on the program level, notably MBAs. To give you a rough idea, among the around 13,000 business schools in the world, about 950 are AACSB accredited, over half of which are in North America; 207 are EQUIS-accredited, with more than half of these in Europe; and 260 AMBA-accredited programs are located in over 75 countries. Comparing both institutional-level accreditations (Zhao and Ferran 2016), EQUIS more intensively analyzes a business school's overall strategy and how it distinguishes itself from other management schools, and focuses more on a school's internationalization; while AACSB looks more at curriculum and syllabus design (cf. aforementioned AoL). In several countries, national accreditations are added to the equation, often even required by the state, and not always consistent with each other. This is particularly salient for cross-border schools such as ESCP (full disclosure: I'm telling you my former problems ☺) that operate in more than one country. To provide you with one example: while the UK accreditor demands that one's own professors' courses and exams be evaluated and checked by a fellow academic in a peer-review manner, the same is expressly prohibited in the German system, which aims to guarantee faculty members' total independence regarding research and teaching. So you can see that lots of creativity is necessary to combine two such systems, as ESCP is compelled to do.

There are four main advantages of pursuing accreditation (Hunt 2014; Noorda 2011; Trapnell 2007; Urgel 2007). Firstly, you get an external assessment of your institution and valuable insights into where you stand on various parameters, ranging from your research strategy and output to teaching quality and innovative pedagogy to your impact on society e.g., sustainability efforts. Secondly, accreditation bodies provide actionable advice on improving your institution. In most cases, you're expected to work on these identified drivers for improvement until the next accreditation round. Thirdly, labels augment your brand and legitimacy, and signal your institution's quality to the market (Pucciarelli and Kaplan 2016, 2017, 2019). Many European business schools publicize their being triple crown accredited, that is, possessing AASCB, AMBA, and EQUIS accreditation, thus belonging to the one percent of business schools worldwide that can claim this achievement. Currently around 100 business schools are triple crowned. Market legitimacy might also have more direct effects, for example, several internationally accredited business schools only enter international exchange partnerships with other similarly accredited business schools, in turn helping to improve your ranking in some of the league tables (see Section 6.2). Finally, administration may use accreditation assessments to justify thus-far unpopular reforms at their institution. They can even implicitly or explicitly try to persuade accreditation teams to point out certain deficiencies or issues in their reports that deans themselves would like to see modified, but that are politically too difficult for them to take on, as they anticipate stakeholders' reactions thereto without formal back-up from a respected third party.

On the down side of accreditation, several issues can be identified in the literature: accreditations in many cases evaluate business schools against inflexible indicators, leading to isomorphism and me-too strategies (e.g., Wilson and Thomas 2012). As such inflexibility cannot do justice to a business school's economic, political, and social environments; some refer to this phenomenon as "accreditocracy" (Avolio and Benzaquen 2020; Perryer and Egan 2015). On the other hand, accreditation might lead to unhealthy competition among business schools, placing unnecessary pressure on some or all of an institution's stakeholders (Guillotin and Mangematin 2015; Prasad, Segarra, and Villanueva 2019). Preparing for and complying with accreditation labels is resource-intensive, resources which might be better channeled into other business school needs and/or activities (Julian and Ofori Dankwa

2006). Above all, however, critique underscores the lack of proof that accreditation leads to an institution's improvement (Stepanovich, Mueller, and Benson 2014; Heriot, Franklin, and Austin 2009). Even worse, some claim that accreditation actually harms a business school's quality, notably due to its emphasis on research output, thereby leading to less emphasis on pedagogy, teaching quality, and educational innovation (Roberts, Johnson, and Groesbeck 2004; Roller, Andrews, and Bovee 2003).

6.2   Rankings' Intention and Impact

Similar to accreditations, as rankings vouch for a business school's quality, they too are an important vector for branding, marketing, and communications (Kaplan and Pucciarelli 2016). Yet, while accreditations actively work to improve business schools by providing them with precise recommendations, rankings do so only indirectly, aiming to incentivize schools to improve on various indicators in order to climb the respective league table. Moreover, while accreditations attempt to consider each institution's specificities, rankings apply the same criteria to all included schools. Therefore, rankings lead to a much higher homogenization of business schools than do accreditations. Most rankings look at several factors and weigh each differently to calculate a school's final composite score, determining an institution's placement on the league table. Data collection varies, from hard financial data to more subjective surveys of students, alumni, professors, and companies that hire graduates. Possible factors that schools can be evaluated on include research output (mostly quantitative, not qualitative), financial return on investment for alumni, quality of instruction, admissions selectivity, student opinions, and post-graduation employment rates.

To illustrate, let's look at the *Financial Times* (FT) Master's in Management annual league table, viewed as the major ranking for European business schools. To enter this ranking, a usual prerequisite is to be AACSB- or EQUIS-accredited, demonstrating one of the interlinkages between rankings and accreditations (*Financial Times* 2022). More than half of a business school's ranking position is the result of questions responded to by the institution's alumni. Criteria look at how quickly alumni found a first job after graduation and their performance in their careers measured three years after having graduated from business school. Absolute salary is measured as well as salary increase over this period. The "value for money" indicator considers salary levels against tuition fees and program duration. Graduates' career progression, international mobility, and program satisfaction are equally assessed. The remaining criteria are the school's student and faculty diversity in terms of gender and nationality, international experience, number of internships and study abroad stays, and the quality of a school's career service.

On the positive side of rankings, four points are worth mentioning (Gibbons, Neumayer, and Perkins 2015; Gregoir 2011): firstly, rankings increase business schools' transparency, rendering them more accountable to their stakeholders. In this vein, rankings are helpful to both candidates and recruiters for broadly evaluating a school against a certain set of indicators, in most cases with comprehensible measures and statistics. Secondly, rankings indirectly incentivize business schools to improve on various criteria. Even remaining stable on a given league table demands great efforts: just as competitors try to climb up a certain ranking, the comfortably ranked institution is compelled to constantly improve so as not to fall in the league table. In some cases, it's even harder to stay on top of the game than to get there: imagine students responding to a question on the quality of their school's career service. If historically, the school ranked in the middle field on this criterion and subsequently made a real effort to improve, students might be inclined to give positive evaluations to praise the endeavor. Now imagine that the school's career service ranks top of the league for years: students duly expect the career service to be top-notch, with even the slightest decrease in service potentially costing the institution several points due to students disappointed by their school's performance on this item. Thirdly, league tables incentivize management schools to think more strategically, prioritize their activities, and decide where to invest their efforts and on what scale they wish to compete. Finally, good ranking positions provide perfect branding, marketing, and communication opportunities and are a point of pride among a school's stakeholders.

Nonetheless, criticism of rankings exists. Firstly, while rankings give the illusion of classifying the same kind of institutions, in some cases they compare apples to oranges. A school might be highly ranked on one scale, but low (if at all) on another scale. This occurs due to each ranking system using a composite score of differing criteria, so that a given ranking may mean differing things on differing tables. The *Financial Times* Master in Management ranking's top positions are recurrently occupied by HEC Paris and the University of St. Gallen. While HEC tuition is approximately €40,000 and its class size is around 500, St. Gallen costs a mere €10,000 with a class size of just above 50. Some "accuse" lower tuition of leading to good evaluations on the value-for-money criterion, with small class sizes resulting from cherry-picking the best candidates. Yet small class sizes and low tuition are recurrently cited by business schools in their marketing brochures, which means that they indeed are an indication of high quality and benefits. The point is that while both programs are ranked highly, the ranking compares differing inputs, leading to potentially quite different study experiences.

Secondly, critics contend that only a minor percentage of the composite scores are comprised of actual pedagogical quality, which is quite difficult to measure. However, this might change with teaching becoming more transparent due to the sector's digitization: imagine, e.g., professors having to produce a three-minute video showcasing their pedagogical skills. Rankings could then randomly choose five videos from each school and evaluate them somehow with, e.g., the help of an external, independent jury. If three minutes does not seem like enough time, institutions could be classified according to the external success of their MOOCs, or evaluated on some of the SPOCs that they use for their teaching. In brief, the online sphere might actually help teaching quality to have more weight in league tables, leading to a rebalancing of the research < > teaching continuum.

Thirdly, some claim that rankings by non-academic institutions, i.e., periodicals, wield too much power in the business school landscape influencing politicians, funding bodies, and opinion leaders in the higher education arena. This in turn might lead to a self-fulfilling prophecy: highly ranked institutions will get more funding, thus able to improve even more, while non-ranked institutions might be left in the dust. The fact is that league tables do have power and have definitely placed certain business schools on top in many people's minds. Even us higher education specialists are surprised whenever a new ranking based on a new calculus comes out that doesn't position the "expected" schools at the top, causing us to doubt even more so the new table's legitimacy. Such an occurrence not only provides food for thought, but might trigger serious questioning regarding rankings.

Fourth, several rankings are criticized for their criteria (i.e., 30% of the FT MiM ranking is based on graduates' salaries, and only 5% on "Aims achieved," i.e., the extent to which alumni feel that their goals were fulfilled by completing a certain Master's program); not to mention statistical methodologies not applying fundamental sample validation and bias reduction techniques that ironically are taught in the marketing research courses at the very business schools that they're evaluating.

6.3   To Improve, Not to Impress

Let's begin with an analogy: while it's every student's objective to obtain their diploma (which is analogous to a business school obtaining an accreditation), ideally make the Dean's list (analogous to a business school reaching a good ranking spot), every educator would state that students should not learn for grades, but rather for life and personal development. Likewise, business schools should pursue accreditation labels and league table placements to improve, not to impress. We saw that accreditations and rankings have several positive effects, but also draw lots of criticism. In my experience, there's only one way to ensure that the positive outweighs the negative of a given school: an institution's leadership has the choice to use rankings and accreditations to genuinely improve, or just to impress, leading management schools to feel compelled to choose between *looking good* and *being good* (Giola and Corley 2002). Pressured by competitors that shine, business schools in some cases seem to be competing more in a Miss Academia pageant than in the Academic Olympics.

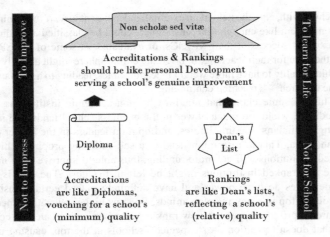

Figure 6.1 A Business School's Learning-for-Life Lesson

Let's look at some of the critiques of accreditations and rankings again. Both lead to some degree of business school homogenization versus differentiation. This is the case if you don't make clear, coherent choices to improve, but instead simply try to do well on quality labels and league tables. Concerning accreditations, in most cases you have a fruitful discussion with the peer-review team on site, enabling you to explain your approach used in your institution and the model upon which it is based. Peer reviewers are experienced academics, and understand whether your choices have logic and consistency. These encounters also enable you to explain the specific economic, political, and social landscape wherein your school navigates. Based on my history, they even like innovation and new ideas, which leaves plenty of room for differentiation within the general business school landscape. But supposing you get reviewers that you feel do not understand you. In that case, there is a security mechanism in place, with in most cases the final decision not made by the review team themselves, but rather by the accreditation body's governance, to whom you can communicate and attempt to convince of an evaluation team's errant assessment. Concerning rankings, the above example comparing HEC Paris with St. Gallen shows that there are many routes to the top: most league tables have elaborate methodologies in place, controlling, e.g., purchasing power versus economic conditions. The oft-claimed consequence of homogenization might therefore not be as pronounced as is claimed (Wojtysiak-Kotlarski 2021).

A further critique concerns rankings and accreditations taking important resources in time and budget that could be used otherwise. While there is truth to this claim, it is only the case if you work toward labels and rankings for the glory and not for the improvement. Above, we had a look at

AACSB's Assurance of Learning standards, stating that their implementation and operation demands a lot of work and commitment. Their aim, however, is to evaluate whether your students master what they are supposed to learn in a specific program, providing a framework helping to achieve this objective. Now suppose you implement AoL criteria only to comply therewith, without really trying to draw benefits from it, i.e., increase your program's quality. In such a case, they indeed are a waste of time (and money). If applied correctly, however, they are effective and efficient, leading to enhanced program quality. If only applied on the surface, they won't work, which might explain why research does not show clear evidence of accreditations improving business schools' quality. Not surprisingly, institutions not genuinely applying an accreditor's criteria likely won't improve much in the end.

Another aspect of rankings is that they require a lot of time to collect and provide the necessary data. However, as aforementioned, they represent marketing and communications means. Therefore, this equation should be easy: if the marketing and communications benefit and value of being ranked in a given league table exceeds the resources expended to get there, then you should participate. If the opposite is the case, then don't. Remember: the aim of budget allocation is quality optimization, notably regarding the student stakeholder group. If rankings augment your brand equity considerably, facilitating graduates' search for good jobs, then your efforts have yielded value. If you believe, however, that you could achieve better value and quality elsewhere with your given resources, then don't hesitate to decline. You don't need to be listed in all rankings across the globe: select those that are worth it for your institution, your specific context, and above all, your students.

Another thing to remember: claims of accreditation and rankings creating unnecessary competition and pressure on various stakeholders should be viewed in context. Again, if benefits exceed costs, go for it. If so, you also need to deploy the necessary resources, including human resources, differently, to avoid overstretching teams in place. If, however, you decide that it's not worth it, then decline. Don't cave to peer pressure that says "We must play the game." Again, a simple (or not-so-simple) cost/benefit analysis will give you the answer. The same goes for criticisms of certain ranking criteria: the FT ranking, e.g., has been accused of placing inordinate weight on alumni salaries as opposed to, e.g., societal or sustainability efforts by institutions. Naturally, the FT could decide to incentivize the latter more. However, it appears that students themselves still feel graduate salaries to be an important criterion when applying to a business school. If the opposite was the case, the FT most likely would have removed the salary criterion out long ago. If your specific target group of potential applicants is less interested in salaries, but more in other "more evolved" domains, then decline this particular ranking. Your target group should easily understand such a decision if you clearly explain the reasons for non-participation; they'll even appreciate such a values-based choice.

While all this advice is more easily written down than translated into action, I think you get my point: it's about improvement, not impressing. It's about quality optimization and consistency in strategy and actions (Cornuel and Hommel 2015; de Onzono and Carmona 2016). Consistency should be applied across the board: some institutions, e.g., contact their alumni prior to their receiving ranking questionnaires, encouraging the latter to "optimize" their responses. If your business school prides itself on educating tomorrow's responsible and ethical leaders, then such an approach would be utterly inconsistent with that message. What would thus-contacted alumni think of their alma mater? That ethical behavior is important until it jeopardizes one's own gain? Lead by example and walk the talk (Maloni et al. 2021), if not spurred by ethics, then at least by brand consistency, whose importance we'll see shortly.

In case your school is not highly ranked or well-accredited, the online world increasingly offers many possibilities to attract potential students nonetheless. You can produce clips of your professors showcasing their pedagogical skills and put them online. Organize online master classes that potential students can audit, giving them a taste of what studying at your institution feels like. Showcase successful careers of your alumni by linking to their LinkedIn accounts or other social media profiles (Kaplan 2012; Kaplan and Haenlein 2010). Use Google's Notable Alumni classification to indicate where selected alumni are. Post Instagram reels or TikTok videos showing students participating in extracurriculars, to mention just a few possibilities. Ultimately, the most valuable decision aid for potential candidates choosing to enroll in a given business school is positive word of mouth from current and former students, whose voices are now far louder thanks to society's digital transformation and the opportunities offered thereby (Kaplan 2021, 2022).

References

Avolio B., Benzaquen J. (2020) Strategic drivers to approach business school's accreditations. *Journal of Education for Business, 95*(8), 519–526.

Cornuel E., Hommel U. (2015) Moving beyond the rhetoric of responsible management education. *Journal of Management Development, 34*(1), 2–15.

De Onzono S. I., Carmona S. (2016) Academic triathlon: Bridging the agora and academia. *Journal of Management Development, 35*(7), 854–865.

Financial Times (2022) Methodology, available online at: https://rankings.ft.com/methodology.

Gibbons S., Neumayer E., Perkins R. (2015) Student satisfaction, league tables, and university applications: Evidence from Britain. *Economics of Education Review, 48*, 148–164.

Giola D. A., Corley K. G. (2002) Being good versus looking good: Business school rankings and the Circean transformation from substance to image. *Academy of Management Learning and Education, 1*(1), 107–120.

Gregoir S. (2011) *Business school rankings and business relevance: An overlooked dimension*. EDHEC Business School.

Guillotin B., Mangematin V. (2015) Internationalization strategies of business schools: How flat is the world? *Thunderbird International Business Review, 57*(5), 343–357.

Heriot K. C., Franklin G., Austin W. W. (2009) Applying for initial AACSB accreditation: An exploratory study to identify costs. *Journal of Education for Business, 84*(5), 283–289.

Hunt S. C. (2014) The value of AACSB business accreditation in selected areas: A review and synthesis. *American Journal of Business Education (AJBE), 8*(1), 23–30.

Jacqmin J., Lefebvre M. (2021) The effect of international accreditations on students' revealed preferences: Evidence from French Business schools. *Economics of Education Review, 85*, 102–192.

Julian S. D., Ofori-Dankwa J. C. (2006) Is accreditation good for the strategic decision making of traditional business schools? *Academy of Management Learning and Education, 5*(2), 225–233.

Kaplan A. (2012) If you love something, let it go mobile: Mobile marketing and mobile social media 4×4. *Business Horizons, 55*(2), 129–139.

Kaplan A. (2018) "A School is a Building that Has 4 Walls – with Tomorrow Inside": Toward the reinvention of the business school. *Business Horizons, 61*(4), 599–608.

Kaplan A. (2021) Higher education at the crossroads of disruption: The university of the 21st century. In *Great Debates in Higher Education*. Emerald Publishing.

Kaplan A. (2022) *Digital transformation and disruption of higher education*. Cambridge University Press.

Kaplan A., Haenlein M. (2010) Users of the world, unite! The challenges and opportunities of social media. *Business Horizons, 53*(1), 59–68.

Kaplan A., Pucciarelli F. (2016) Contemporary challenges in higher education – Three E's for education: Enhance, embrace, expand. *IAU Horizons*, International Universities Bureau of the United Nations, 21(4), 25–26.

Maloni M. J., Palmer T. B., Cohen M., Gligor D. M., Grout J. R., Myers R. (2021) Decoupling responsible management education: Do business schools walk their talk? *International Journal of Management Education, 19*(1), 100456.

Noorda S. (2011) Future business schools. *Journal of Management Development, 30*(5), 519–525.

Perryer C., Egan V. (2015) Business school accreditation in developing countries: A case in Kazakhstan. *Journal of Eastern European and Central Asian Research, 2*(2), 11.

Prasad A., Segarra P., Villanueva C. E. (2019) Academic life under institutional pressures for AACSB accreditation: Insights from faculty members in Mexican business schools. *Studies in Higher Education, 44*(9), 1605–1618.

Pucciarelli F., Kaplan A. (2016) Competition and strategy in higher education: Managing complexity and uncertainty. *Business Horizons, 59*(3), 311–320.

Pucciarelli F., Kaplan A. (2017) Le Università Europee oggi: Sfide e nuove strategie. *Economia & Management*, gennaio/febbraio, *1*, 85–95.

Pucciarelli F., Kaplan A. (2019) "Competition in higher education" in B. Nguyen, T. C. Melewar, and J. Hemsley-Brown (eds.), *Strategic brand management in higher education*. Routledge.

Roberts W. A., Johnson R., Groesbeck J. (2004) A faculty perspective on the impact of AACSB accreditation. *Academy of Educational Leadership Journal*, *8*(1), 111–125.

Roller R. H., Andrews B. K., Bovee A. L. (2003) Specialized accreditation of business schools: A comparison of alternative costs, benefits, and motivations. *Journal of Education for Business*, *78*(4), 197–204.

Stepanovich P., Mueller J., Benson D. (2014) AACSB accreditation and possible unintended consequences: A Deming view. *Journal of Education for Business*, *89*(2), 103–109.

Trapnell J. E. (2007) AACSB International Accreditation: The value proposition and a look to the future. *Journal of Management Development*, *26*(1), 67–72.

Urgel J. (2007) EQUIS accreditation: Value and benefits for international business schools. *Journal of Management Development*, *26*(1), 73–83.

Wilson D. C., Thomas, H. (2012) The legitimacy of the business of business schools: What's the future? *Journal of Management Development*, *31*, 368–376.

Wojtysiak-Kotlarski M. (2021) Benefits for business schools from top international accreditations: Lessons-learned from AACSB and EQUIS projects. *Organization Review*, *1*(972), 17–24.

Zhao J., Ferran C. (2016) Business school accreditation in the changing global marketplace: A comparative study of agencies and their competitive strategies. *Journal of International Education in Business*, *9*(1), 52–69.

7 Business Schools
Spot Your Niche and Point of Difference

Have you ever wondered why many consumers go crazy every time Apple launches a new product? When it comes to Apple, we expect nothing less than fashionable design, innovation, and the latest technological advances. This is what the Apple brand evokes. Some iPhones cost more than a laptop. Consumers are willing to pay premium prices for Apple's most recent version, despite the fact that the difference in production costs between the highest- and lowest-priced iPhone is almost negligible. This is only one result of successful branding and differentiation from competitors, best illustrated with one of Apple's former slogans, "Think Different."

Harvard Business School, IMD, INSEAD, LBS, RSM, Saïd Business School, and the Wharton School are very strong brands and well-known actors in the business school landscape. A strong, well-known brand is undeniably a huge advantage, and notoriety and brand equity are two of the main drivers of a management school's success (Siebert and Martin 2013). Ask yourself what the above-cited business schools are known for beyond the fact that they are top tier. Is there any specific aspect that they immediately call to mind? Especially for schools not belonging to the top tier, a me-too approach and strategy of non-differentiation, i.e., not "Thinking Different," might become quite dangerous in a future wherein the aforementioned best of the best are just a click away, digitally speaking. A more successful strategy might be finding your institution's niche and point of difference, and actively engaging in branding it (Nguyen, Melewar, and Hemsley-Brown 2019, Kaplan 2021 a, b).

Business schools increasingly need to clearly distinguish themselves from each other, i.e., they need to spot their niche. Students and faculty enabled to study and work remotely need convincing reasons to choose a specific management institution instead of simply joining one of the top-ranked, big brand's online programs. Business schools also need to showcase their positive points of difference from alternative, less academic providers that offer shorter and less costly programs, such as ThePowerMBA or LinkedIn Learning. While such brand differentiation and positioning are of the essence, several limitations and obstacles on the way need to be considered. Brand consistency is an additional important marketing tool. Once a certain positioning has been

DOI: 10.4324/9781003343509-7

decided upon, a business school should firmly stick to it. Successful branding must go beyond a simple communications and marketing strategy, and integrate all business school activities coherently and consistently. If skilled in one's branding, so-called brand advocates will emerge, defend, and advocate for their alma mater. Not only can alumni be effective brand ambassadors, but all business school stakeholders should be considered potential proponents of one's brand and treated as such, within certain limits and boundaries (Kaplan 2021b).

7.1 Brand Differentiation and Positioning

Most business schools know that their brand (Hemsley-Brown and Goonawardana 2007) is essential when, e.g., attracting candidates to their various programs (all the more so when tuition is high), as a student's choice of school will become part of their CV and personal brand identity once entering the job market. A business school also relies on its brand when recruiting new faculty members, searching for partnerships with companies, or engaging in agreements with partner institutions. People prefer to study or work at and with organizations that are well-known (Bock, Poole, and Joseph 2014; Friga, Bettis, and Sullivan 2003).

Not only does higher education's digital transformation render it even more important to have a reputed brand (Kaplan 2022), but business schools in particular should pursue a strategy of clear brand differentiation (Aaker 2003; Caruana, Pitt, Berthon, and Page 2009). Think of research-active faculty required only to teach a very limited number of hours per year, many of these potentially online (cf. Chapter 2): they no longer need to live where their business school is located. They can commute a couple of times a year and work remotely the rest of the time, i.e., do their research anywhere in the world. If brands are similar, often the only differentiation is the offered salary and the institution's position in league tables (cf. Chapter 6). Yet not everybody can get the number one ranking spot (which in any case should not be an aim in itself) and pay top dollar or euro salaries. The more differentiated and unique an institution, appealing to a target group with its particular brand characteristics, the more it can compete in such a market.

Students, too, could decide to stay home and study online. Covid-19 strengthened online education and rendered the latter an acknowledged and established phenomenon. The world of e-learning expands the reach of programs and training so that students from anywhere can attend courses anytime they want to be taught by top faculty members worldwide. Remember Laurie Pickard, who curated an MBA from the best business schools worldwide (Pickard 2017)? If ranking positions are the only differentiating element, students can ask why they should attend a lower-ranked school over a higher-ranked one (Kethüda 2022). They might prefer getting an online degree from a reputed school over an in-person education from a less-known school. Alternatively, they also might choose the significantly cheaper and more quickly obtainable certificates from edtech and big tech.

If truth be told, neither in the past did students base their choice of business schools entirely on ranking positions, but rather tried to get a feel for a certain institution during campus visits, admissions interviews, or by looking at the various information one could find about a certain program and school on- and offline. They searched for differentiators of the various schools out there (Caruana, Pitt, Berthon, and Page 2009). Yet in the future, with the landscape ever more competitive, differentiation must be stronger and branding much more distinct. Brand differentiation and positioning will help business schools cut through the recently accentuated digital clutter.

A clear differentiation strategy moreover forges firm attachment of a business school's various stakeholders to their alma mater. While it is true that by defining a distinct brand with a clearly distinguished mission and differentiation, you might lose those professors, students, and alumni who are not supportive of your newly created brand identity and attributes, it is also true that those who remain and especially those who join due to your positioning and differentiation, will be that much more loyal to your institution (Stephenson and Yerger 2014). It is easier and more appealing to be identified with a genuine mission and a clear objective than to a business school whose differentiation rests on being the best in the world, country, or region, especially as league tables might change their criteria, subsequently significantly changing schools' rankings.

Graduates want to be proud of something; they want to be able to tell a story about their alma mater, and they want to be part of a like-minded community…so give them one. Attached stakeholders will go the extra mile for you and act as brand advocates and ambassadors (Stephenson and Yerger 2014). Moreover, clear branding and differentiation enable asking price premiums, (Davcik and Sharma 2015) i.e., higher tuition, which is obviously of particular importance vis-à-vis non-academic actors swamping the market with low-cost training and courses. In marketing jargon, the limit to such price premiums is called *perceived price fairness* (Xia, Monroe, and Cox 2004), i.e., students who feel their tuition fees are not justified might attend a business school, but their attachment to it will be low, with the alma mater missing out on all the advantages of loyal students and alumni.

Various possibilities for differentiating and positioning exist. Concerning less academic actors from ed and big tech, the business schools' branding should focus on the advantages of their programs over those of non-traditional providers, such as the following: traditional business schools have a clear society-wide, non-commercial purpose, which can be a strong argument for educational quality not having to look at profits, but rather optimizing academic quality. They often are creators of knowledge via their (hopefully relevant) research output, i.e., produce the latest theories and concepts versus practitioners who graduated years or decades ago and whose knowledge may be somewhat outdated; faculty at business schools are experts in their domains, often on a world-class level; professors and their management institutions are specialists in designing programs and curricula, and know how to progressively and optimally improve a student's insights, skills, and competences.

When differentiating from other business schools, the respective institution can choose a specific realm on which to focus, such as sustainability (Pucciarelli and Kaplan 2021, 2022), digitization (Kaplan and Haenlein 2016), and the most profound international or multicultural experience. It can choose a specific pedagogical approach, such as the case study approach, or highly interdisciplinary teaching and learning (Kaplan 2021d). It can boast the best scientific research in a certain (highly relevant) domain. It can offer more customization (while keeping complexity to a minimum) than the competition in terms of number of electives or the pace of one's studies, thus allowing, e.g., for part-time employ alongside one's studies. It can focus on training the best future employees for a certain industry, such as the fashion, logistics, or hospitality sector.

A chosen differentiation should first of all be difficult for competitors to copy, which is not easy to achieve: few business schools have unique characteristics that no one can copy, as they're rather generic in nature. That makes it all the more important, secondly, to go all the way with one's selected differentiation to be credible on your chosen positioning. For instance, several schools claim to focus on sustainability, with many simply jumping on the bandwagon, yet very few are credible and legitimate in this area. Also, coming back to the uniqueness aspect, ask whether sustainability, for example, will be differentiating enough if many actors pursue the same branding. This isn't to say that sustainability is not important; it just might not be suitable as *your* main differentiation characteristic. Moreover, a good differentiation must thirdly attract a business school's stakeholders. Will a certain branding attract new students and executive education participants? Will faculty and staff be excited to work for such a business school? Fourthly, good positioning should be easy to understand and simple to communicate: simplicity leads to market exposure and visibility.

Finally, it is the students' employment market that ultimately decides whether one's branding is a success. Would an employer be able to tell what a business school's brand stands for? Are a given school's alumni more competent in the areas upon which their alma mater's brand is differentiated? Are employers actually in need of graduates with those skills? If companies have difficulty distinguishing successful graduates of alternative provider programs from business school graduates, then the entire sector might have to rethink its strategies (Kaplan 2021 f).

7.2   Brand Coherence and Consistency

Apple's message is always consistent regardless of where you encounter their brand. Their communications, products, stores, and employees all represent the same message and ethos. Consistency is the key to effective branding and differentiation. A successful differentiation and branding strategy go a lot further than communication and marketing, a fact often not recognized by business schools worldwide. Branding touches on the product, the institution, the personnel – literally on everything associated with the brand. If a business school claims, for example, to be a strong advocate for inter- and multidisciplinary education, one should not be able to find a single program in its catalogue that does not reflect a strong interdisciplinary approach. If an institution positions itself as the digital transformation hub, then several courses should at least partly take place in the metaverse (Kaplan and Haenlein 2009 a,b,c; Malagocka, Mazurek, and Kaplan 2022). These are just two examples of an institution being strongly positioned in a given realm.

To extend the sustainability example (Traca 2022), imagine a business school advocating for sustainability everywhere in their marketing and promotion material. Then imagine students not receiving any instruction on sustainability during their studies. Imagine faculty members flying to scientific conferences, even though their destinations are reachable by train. Imagine the same business school not recycling its waste, not installing a sustainable heating and cooling system…you get the idea. Such an institution most likely will soon be accused of greenwashing, lose credibility with its internal stakeholders, and, thanks to social media (Kaplan 2012, Kaplan and Haenlein 2010), its external stakeholders will also learn of this inconsistency – if not hypocrisy – so detrimental to the school's brand image.

If you place sustainability at the top of your agenda, you must ensure that academic, operational, and institutional matters align therewith. Does each program teach about sustainability? Are your campus operations sustainable? Do your institutional partnerships reflect your dedication to sustainability? From experience, I know that some aspects of walking the talk are harder than others. For example, it's relatively easy to introduce recycling on campus, as nobody feels limited in their options by such a move. However, removing meat from the meal plan and/or replacing it with more sustainable food options is likely to lead to complaints, petitions, and stress-producing press attention. I recall having been accused of forcing others to eat certain foods when I decided to go all-vegetarian for a garden party that my school organized. While in this case it was a no-brainer for me to stick to my decision, I admittedly paused before ultimately deciding to go meatless at all of the school's official events thereafter. Despite this hesitation, we never regretted this move. Leadership must stand strong in such situations, proof of the school's dedication to a chosen positioning, as at stake are brand coherence and credibility (Kaplan 2021 e, g, h).

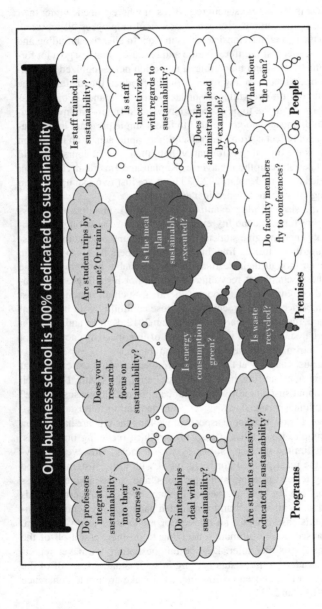

Figure 7.1 Brand Coherence: The Sustainability Example

Indeed, brand differentiation can be a challenging endeavor. While a business school's leadership should provide direction, deciding on a new positioning or a more pronounced brand differentiation preferably employs a bottom-up approach, as a branding strategy without backing from a school's main stakeholders will most certainly fail (Chapleo 2010). You need everyone on board: faculty must be convinced of adapting their courses and research to the new positioning while guaranteeing their academic freedom, i.e., in no case compel them to mold their academic work to a certain branding but rather, they need to voluntarily join the endeavor. Alumni as well need to back the positioning, which might take artful persuasion if it deviates strongly from a school's previous branding strategy. Employers must be enthused about hiring graduates from a school with a certain branding and differentiation strategy, and so forth.

A clear differentiation strategy will likely mean recruiting professors whose profile fits the institution's positioning, as opposed to those with the highest research output, unless their research topic aligns with the institution's branding. Wisely chosen professors can support your positioning strongly with their research and resulting PR. Clear differentiation likely also means that a business school's leadership will have to make tough decisions to eliminate some programs, initiatives, or traditions. This must of course be done delicately in an effort to least offend both external and internal stakeholders, who after all comprise your team. An open and transparent discussion with and explanation to all stakeholders is a must, and should persuade them to get on board with your branding strategy. Those who feel involved will want to be part of major strategic moves.

Examples of difficult implementations of differentiation strategies abound: when ESCP Business School, at that time only in Paris, wanted to strengthen its European positioning, i.e., as the European School of Commerce (Paris), it merged with EAP (the École des Affaires de Paris), already present in several cities across Europe, many key stakeholders of both schools opposed it. Today, the six ESCP campuses (in Berlin, London, Madrid, Paris, Turin, and Warsaw) are one of the school's main strengths and a clear trademark (Kaplan 2018). Whatever your school's unique strengths are, these should manifest in its academic programs, including lifelong learning. I speak from experience, as I served as ESCP's Director of Brand and Communications for a couple of years. Only major brands can succeed without differentiation, by positioning themselves as simply *the best*. Again, top ranking spots are not set in stone. Accordingly, good brand differentiation beyond simply being No. 1 might be the more stable and long-term strategy.

Some institutions are already adopting such a strategy, although we can always go further. Aalto Business School in Helsinki, e.g., bills itself as "a multidisciplinary community of bold thinkers, where science and art meet technology and business. We are committed to identifying and solving grand societal challenges, and building an innovative future provides students with multidisciplinary learning experiences and opportunities." Aalto's inception itself is a multidisciplinary adventure, as it is the result of a 2010 merger of three institutions teaching differing academic disciplines: Helsinki University of Technology, Helsinki School of Economics, and University of Art and Design Helsinki. The merger's explicit intention was to pursue an inter- and multidisciplinary approach to teaching and research, bringing together management, technology, and the arts. Before the merger, faculty from all three disciplines engaged in discussions and exchanges to analyze the opportunities and challenges of such collaboration, which is considered an important milestone in the project's successful implementation (Kaplan 2021c).

ESMOD International, the world's first fashion school (est. 1841), is another example of a highly differentiated management school focusing on apparel. In 1989, ESMOD broadened its activities, which until then exclusively focused on fashion design and creation, and launched its fashion business school division. In its course catalogue, one finds fashion management, and fashion marketing, alongside courses such as eco-responsibility, innovation, and the apparel business's digital transformation. For a Master's degree, approximately two years of internships in the clothing industry are required. Moreover, every ESMOD business student must partner with a student from ESMOD's fashion design division to market and manage the latter's own created fashion line. When you enter ESMOD's campus, you feel and see that it's about learning the business of fashion. It's located at the edge of Pantin, a suburb of Paris, which has become a hub for brands such as Hermès, Chanel, and Gucci, all in close proximity. Two well-known alumni are fashion designer Christophe Decarnin, and Olivier Rousteing, creative director of Balmain.

The Kühne Logistics University (KLU), a state-recognized higher education institution based in Hamburg, Germany, and founded in 2010, is a final example of a school centered around one specific area of expertise. KLU is supported by the Kühne Foundation and its sole benefactor Klaus-Michael Kühne, a German businessman and entrepreneur who, among others, is the honorary chair and majority shareholder of the multinational logistics company Kühne + Nagel. KLU, therefore, focuses its teaching and research on logistics, transportation, and supply chain management, a sector that accounts for roughly ten percent of the global GDP and, equally, ten percent of global CO_2 emissions. Without substantial change, freight and transportation will become the highest greenhouse gas emitting sector by 2050 (Rogelj, Shindell, Jiang, et al. 2018). Hence, increasing supply chain efficiency through AI, IoT, and blockchain technologies can significantly improve the world's environmental sustainability. This is only one of several illustrations of why there is a need to teach and research supply chain management, its digital transformation, and eco-responsibility and have one institution entirely dedicated to this purpose. Given the breadth and size of the sector, as well as its transversal nature that spans most countries and industries, students do not seem to miss a broader focus. KLU was awarded studyportals.com's 2021 Global Student Satisfaction Award, solely based on a university's student reviews.

Given this chapter is about branding and as KLU's current president, I should additionally point out that the Kühne Logistics University is located in Hamburg's HafenCity, one of Europe's top three largest seaports, that Germany regularly ranks No. 1 in the World Bank's Logistics Performance Index, and that, therefore, there is no better place to acquire a strong operations mindset in the world.

7.3 Brand Advocates and Ambassadors

Apple's branding turns brand loyalty into brand advocacy, encouraging customers to become active ambassadors for the consumer electronics giant. Apple clients are loyal and talk about, promote, and advocate for "their" brand. Marketers would calculate Apple's net-promoter score, i.e. the likelihood that a customer would recommend a product or service to a friend or colleague (Reichheld 2003). Customers engage in word-of-mouth marketing and thus become influencers, happy to tell the world about "their" brand. These brand advocates are invaluable, as they're extremely credible in transmitting a brand's message. People prefer listening to brand advocates over an institution's official communications, which are considered less trustworthy and authentic. Advocates are intrinsically motivated to advertise a brand – for free – simply because they love it. They participate simply because they enjoy being part of the story and the brand, and want others to benefit therefrom. Likewise, although being a fan of their branding strategy, I'm not paid to promote Apple, business schools would do well to take a page from Apple's book.

To turn stakeholders into brand advocates, you need to make them feel appreciated and valued. You need to give them the feeling that they're special to you. To do so, you need first to go the extra mile yourself: you need to engage with them on a personal and emotional level. Wharton went so far as to create the position of Dean of Happiness, in charge of defending students' interests facing various stakeholders. While not called that at ESCP, we came close to creating such a position, which was filled by Zana Rachedi who was hired for this newly created position by ESCP's Dean at the time, the avantgardiste Pascal Morand. Zana managed to create incredible relationships with our students, who trusted her with their concerns and issues at school, and in some cases beyond. When she could, she took care of it. When she couldn't or disagreed with the students, she honestly told them what to expect and why she couldn't or wouldn't help them in specific cases. Regardless, she always gave them valuable advice on how best to deal with a given situation. When Zana left, it became obvious that her vacated position requires specific skill sets that apparently are difficult to find. Therefore with Zana Rachedi's (and Pascal Morand's) departure, unfortunately, the position was not retained.

The clearer and more coherent a branding strategy, the easier it is to provide stakeholders with information about the brand, stories, and media content to share. Ideally, such content is adapted to the respective stakeholder group, e.g., faculty communicates with different people than do students and alumni. The more adapted to their respective conversations, the easier for them to promote your brand. Moreover, you need to simplify communications for your brand advocates. They can only talk about your brand if you let them know its characteristics and what message you ideally want them to transmit and share (Barron 2015). As a marketer, I would go for the KISS principle, i.e., keep it short and simple. Encourage them to engage in word-of-mouth communication. Calls to action are effective as well. Above all, thank them for being your brand advocates. Always remind yourself that they do not need to talk about you: they're doing it of their own volition, as they like and appreciate you.

Students can be strong brand advocates, by, e.g., promoting the school via their extracurriculars. Alumni can be your best ambassadors, boosting your marketing campaign and messages to coworkers, colleagues, friends, and family members; it's no surprise that referrals from students and alumni count for over half of incoming students in many programs. Professors are excellent brand advocates as well, as they talk about their research and about what is happening in their business school. Are they aware of its brand characteristics? Do they know about their institution's latest success? To find out, do the elevator test: ask your faculty members how they would describe your business school in 30 seconds. You might be surprised by the answers. Ask them how their research fits with the school's branding. Are they able to respond? If not, revise and improve your internal communications. The same applies to support staff and non-academic personnel, who often feel underappreciated and undervalued. How would they talk about their employer? What would they emphasize when talking about you?

Finally, probably a business school's most visible brand advocate is its dean (or at least it should be), part of whose job is building relationships and bridges with external and internal stakeholders. People prefer talking to a face as opposed to an institution, so the dean must be authentic and credible in her message. People also seek genuine interest, not talking points that they could get by reading the institution's website. Let me tell you an anecdote: for quite some time, I have advocated combining management with sustainability, which led to organizing an annual conference on that topic aiming at inspiring students to lead a more sustainable lifestyle and to take sustainability into account in their future decision-making as managers and entrepreneurs. Accordingly, I stressed the importance of sustainability in my keynote speech. After the conference, a student approached me to ask whether I was actually doing myself what I'd just talked about. This moment was very embarrassing for me, as I was not. Can you imagine the potential detrimental effect thereof on an organization's brand image? The student easily could have shared my incoherence on social media, which luckily for me he did not, and for which

I'm still thankful. A year later, at the same conference, I again talked about sustainability, this time focusing on my difficulties and barriers to leading a more sustainable lifestyle. That speech was a lot more powerful and credible, as it was still aligned with the school's branding and positioning, but was much more authentic and genuine.

References

Aaker D. A. (2003) The power of the branded differentiator. *MIT Sloan Management Review*, *45*(1), 83–87.

Barron J. (2015) Building a chain of success in marketing higher education: The alumni connection. *Industrial and Commercial Training*, *47*(5), 253–256.

Bock D. E., Poole S. M., Joseph M. (2014) Does branding impact student recruitment? A critical evaluation. *Journal of Marketing for Higher Education*, *24*(1), 11–21.

Caruana A., Pitt L. F., Berthon P., Page M. (2009) Differentiation and silver medal winner effects. *European Journal of Marketing*, *43*(11/12), 1365–1377.

Chapleao C. (2010) What defines "successful" university brands? *International Journal of Public Sector Management*, *23*(2), 169–183.

Davcik N. S., Sharma P. (2015) Impact of product differentiation, marketing investments, and brand equity on pricing strategies. *European Journal of Marketing*, *9*(5/6), 760–781.

Friga P. N., Bettis R. A., Sullivan R. S. (2003) Changes in graduate management education and new business school strategies for the 21st century. *Academy of Management Learning and Education*, *2*(3), 233–249.

Hemsley-Brown J., Goonawardana S. (2007) Brand harmonization in the international higher education market, *Journal of Business Research*, *60*(9), 942–948.

Kaplan A. (2012) If you love something, let it go mobile: Mobile marketing and mobile social media 4×4. *Business Horizons*, *55*(2), 129–139.

Kaplan A. (2018) Toward a theory of European business culture: The case of management education at the ESCP Europe Business School. In S. Gabriele, R. Monica, L. Johan (eds.), *The Routledge companion to European business* (pp. 113–124). Routledge.

Kaplan A. (2021a) Branding and bonding: The key to competing in the digital age. EAIE – European Association for International Education, July 6, 2021, available online at https://www.eaie.org/blog/branding-bonding-competing-digital-age .html.

Kaplan A. (2021b) Business schools, differentiate yourselves! *AASCB Insights*, June 8, 2021, available online at https://www.aacsb.edu/insights/2021/june/business -schools-differentiate-yourselves.

Kaplan A. (2021c) Higher education at the crossroads of disruption: The university of the 21st century. In *Great debates in higher education*. Emerald Publishing.

Kaplan A. (2021d) Multi- and interdisciplinarity empowered and entailed by business schools' digitalization. *efmdglobal.org*, April 29, 2021, available online at https:// blog.efmdglobal.org/2021/04/29/multi-and-interdisciplinarity-business-schools -digitalisation/.

Kaplan A. (2021e) *Prepare for student sustainability demands to go through the roof.* The Times Higher Education, October 19 2021, available online at https://www

.timeshighereducation.com/campus/prepare-student-sustainability-demands-go -through-roof.

Kaplan A. (2021f) *Professionals need to keep their skills fresh. Will they turn to higher ed?* Harvard Business Publishing, September 17, 2021, available online at https:// www.hbsp.harvard.edu/inspiring-minds/professionals-need-to-keep-their-skills -fresh-will-they-turn-to-higher-ed/?ab=top_nav.

Kaplan A. (2021g) Slowly but surely: Business schools boost sustainability. *Emerald Blog Post*, February 2 2021, available online at https://www.emeraldgrou ppublishing.com/opinion-and-blog/slowly-surely-business-schools-boost -sustainability.

Kaplan A. (2021h) The 21st-century university: Societal and sustainable, responsible research in business and management, RRBM. *www.rrbm.network*, May 7, 2021, available online at https://www.rrbm.network/the-21st-century-university -societal-and-sustainable-andreas-kaplan/.

Kaplan A. (2022) *Digital transformation and disruption of higher education.* Cambridge University Press.

Kaplan A., Haenlein M. (2009a) Consumer use and business potential of virtual worlds: The case of Second Life. *International Journal on Media Management, 11*(3/4), 93–101.

Kaplan A., Haenlein M. (2009b) Consumers, companies and virtual social worlds: A qualitative analysis of Second Life. *Advances in Consumer Research, 36*(1), 873–874.

Kaplan A., Haenlein M. (2009c) The fairyland of Second Life: Virtual social worlds and how to use them. *Business Horizons, 52*(6), 563–572.

Kaplan A., Haenlein M. (2010) Users of the world, unite! The challenges and opportunities of social media. *Business Horizons, 53*(1), 59–68.

Kaplan A., Haenlein M. (2016) Higher education and the digital revolution: About MOOCs, SPOCs, social media, and the Cookie Monster. *Business Horizons, 59*(4), 441–450.

Kethüda O. (2022) Evaluating the influence of university ranking on the credibility and perceived differentiation of university brands. *Journal of Marketing for Higher Education*, 1–18.

Malagocka K., Mazurek G., Kaplan A. (2022) Virtual worlds, virtual reality, and augmented reality: Review, synthesis, and research agenda. In Z. Yan (ed.), *The Cambridge handbook of cyber behavior.* Cambridge University Press.

Nguyen B., Melewar T. C., Hemsley-Brown J. (2019) *Strategic brand management in higher education.* Routledge.

Pickard L. (2017) *Don't pay for your MBA: The faster, cheaper, better way to get the business education you need.* AMACOM.

Pucciarelli F., Kaplan A. (2021) From narrative to action: Are business schools walking the talk of responsible management education? *efmdglobal.org*, June 28, 2021, available online at https://blog.efmdglobal.org/2021/06/28/from-narrative-to -action-are-business-schools-walking-the-talk-of-responsible-management -education/.

Pucciarelli F., Kaplan A. (2022) A transition to a hybrid teaching model as a step forward toward responsible management education? *Journal of Global Responsibility, 3*(1), 7–20.

Reichheld F. F. (2003) The one number you need to grow. *Harvard Business Review, 81*(12), 46–54.

Rogelj J., Shindell D., Jiang K., et al. (2018) Mitigation pathways compatible with 1.5°C in the context of sustainable development. In *Global warming of 1.5°C* (pp. 93–174). Intergovernmental Panel on Climate Change.

Siebert S., Martin G. (2013) Reputational challenges for business schools: A contextual perspective. *Education and Training, 55*(4/5), 429–444.

Stephenson A. L., Yerger D. B. (2014) Does brand identification transform alumni into university advocates? *International Review on Public and Non-Profit Marketing, 11*(3), 243–262.

Traca D. (2022) Transforming business schools into lighthouses of hope for a sustainable future. In E. Cornuel (ed.), *Business school leadership and crisis exit planning: Global Deans' contributions on the occasion of the 50th anniversary of the EFMD* (pp. 154–178). Cambridge University Press.

Xia L., Monroe K. B., Cox J. L. (2004) The price is unfair! A conceptual framework of price unfairness perceptions. *Journal of Marketing, 68*, 1–5.

8 Business Schools' Survival Based on Bonding and Building

Community building is a strategy centered on bringing people together over a topic that is aligned with a specific brand in a highly engaging, yet non-intrusive manner (McAlexander, Schouten, and Koenig 2002; Muniz and O'Guinn 2001). Alongside branding and differentiation (cf. Chapter 7), community building is another marketing concept applied to business schools to help them thrive in the digital environment. This book being written by a marketing academic is not a coincidence, and moreover confirms the adage "Cobbler, stick to your trade." Regardless, psychology research shows that connecting with others who are like-minded is more rewarding to us than are financial incentives, power, or fame. The sense of togetherness necessitates a strong brand to which stakeholders can relate and to which they feel connected (Balmer, Liao, and Wang 2010).

To illustrate a highly successful brand community, let's once again look to Apple (last time, I promise!). While higher education certainly differs from consumer electronics, Apple's brand community can serve as an example for business schools. To comprehend why Apple's customers form a solid "fan community," understand that Apple has become part of their identity: Apple regularly engages with its customers and is involved in their lives. Apple provides its clients with a platform and a place to meet and hang out. In other words, Apple creates an entire experience around its brand, and consequently, Apple customers act as brand ambassadors, as they want to disseminate their community spirit to the world. If you've ever made a negative remark about Apple to one of its loyal customers, then you understand the strength and power of brand communities.

Community building, bonding, and fostering attachment among and across all of a business school's stakeholders constitutes a substantial barrier to competition. A community is stronger when subgroup membership, e.g., the faculty or student body, transposes itself into belonging to a single, undivided group-without-borders. Alongside a variety of community-building activities, strengthening lifelong learning is of specific interest. Early-life degrees should seamlessly lead to continuous education, a highly effective driver of community spirit. Lifelong learning liaisons should replace the current transactional system of study > work > retire. Finally, while buildings

DOI: 10.4324/9781003343509-8

might be considered increasingly redundant against the backdrop of intensified digitalization, believe it or not, they are components of effective community building. More than just brick-and-mortar, real estate has become more critical than ever in the higher education sector. With online courses available, stakeholders have less reason to come to campus. They only will do so if buildings are welcoming and encourage working, networking, and hanging out together. The successful business school of the future needs to have seamless transitions between the physical and the virtual environments (Kaplan and Haenlein 2009 a,b,c; Malogocka, Mazurek, and Kaplan 2022).

8.1 Community Building Offsets Competition

Building strong communities among all business school stakeholders is a protective measure against an increasingly competitive management education landscape. Community members who are strongly attached to their business school will be loyal to it, defend it, and advocate for it (Kaplan 2021a,b). Attachment, however, is forged by experiences and exchanges, which often occur outside the classroom (Dass, Kabra, Saxena, and Vinay 2020). With increasing numbers of online courses, coffee with classmates, or with one's professor, is a decreasing phenomenon. Business schools therefore need to actively foster opportunities for such bonding and exchanges (Petriglieri and Petiglieri 2010). One possibility for doing so is the integration of group work into the course syllabus. Another is actively supporting and facilitating extracurriculars (Archbold and O'Hagan 2011). Finally, field trips are often mentioned by (former) students as one of the most memorable experiences of their time at university. Budgetary considerations notwithstanding, such trips should be part of any curriculum, as the memories they create serve to attach their participants to their alma mater (Andre, Williams, Schwartz, and Bullard 2017). One doesn't have to travel far to have an exciting experience: a neighboring country or even domestic travel can be just as much of a success. For sustainability reasons, domestic destinations might in any case be the preferred option.

Students become alumni. To forge good relationships therewith, students should be considered alumni the moment they enter the institution for the first time. If students are not convinced of a business school's genuine interest in them during their studies, it will be hard to persuade them to become involved alumni after they graduate. Moreover, engaging in relationship building is far easier done with students, to which the institution has immediate access, than with alumni, with whom contact is far less regular. Routinely, alumni are organized in alumni associations, which serve as bridges between the school and its former students. Accordingly, alumni associations must be included in the institution's important decisions. Moreover, remember that not all alumni are necessarily members of the alumni association, as the latter are often still run based on membership fees. Nonetheless, non-member alumni should not be neglected, as they are valuable assets to a business school as well, if there is a system in place that enables getting in touch with them.

Faculty also must be an integral part of the business school community. To attract a promising professor demands some heavy lifting and effort: such a candidate will likely be promised a strongly reduced teaching load, allowing him or her plenty of time to conduct research (cf. Chapter 2). However, when it comes down to it, the publish-or-perish directive does not foster attachment. Firstly, it leaves the professor working on an inherently solitary activity, which is not a very community-fostering experience. Additionally, you're sending the message that if he or she doesn't pass the publication threshold, s/he is no longer welcome at the institution, regardless of what else s/he contributes or how much commitment and investment s/he shows.

It is thus not surprising that professors who manage to publish articles, i.e., improve their employability, benefit therefrom and subsequently leave for the highest-paying business school. Thus a better strategy might be to attach them to your business school from the outset, look beyond their publication record, and integrate them as valuable colleagues, significantly increasing the chances of counting them among the school's long-time faculty. Retaining faculty over time also helps community building across other stakeholder groups: think of former students who were fans of a certain course and professor, coming back as alumni. They might be able to reconnect with their favorite instructors at a social event or on more formal occasions. These things count, more than we realize.

Finally, once again, don't forget about the non-academic staff (cf. Chapter 1), who are valuable community members. Do you award a Teacher of the Year Award? Do you also recognize the best non-academic staff member? Do you organize events only for alumni, events dedicated to students, or events reserved for faculty only? Do you also organize events restricted to only administrative staff members? Perhaps you do, or not. In the best case, everybody feels a part of the school: not strictly as students or alumni, or professors, nor as leadership, or administrative staff. Only as supporters and advocates of their business school are they all part of the same community. The more events you host to which all stakeholders are invited, the more opportunities you give everybody to meet everybody, the more everyone will feel like one united community.

Most likely, however, subgroups will persist. To feel appreciated as community members, they must have the sense that their voices count, and that no one stakeholder group is considered more important than another. It is the dean's job to balance and maneuver between the various stakeholder groups. If priority should at all be given to one stakeholder group, it should be the students, as student-centricity will be key in academia's future in the (digital) landscape that lies ahead.

On the other hand, making students happy at other stakeholders' expense will not result in community spirit, and consequently will also be detrimental for the students. In other words, a happy faculty and a happy administrative team will lead to happy students and future alumni. Do not read "make students happy" to mean making concessions on academic matters. Pedagogy should be both demanding and help students become great managers and entrepreneurs. Students enroll in business school to have an experience, of which top-notch pedagogy and challenging academic requirements must be a part. Obviously, everything should be done so that students are supported and helped to be able to perform well academically; this is, after all, what family or a nurturing mother does, as *alma mater* means in Latin.

The dean should not be involved in community building only when difficult decisions are made. He or she, together with the entire leadership team, can create strong community spirit by simply showing interest in the stakeholders. This must go beyond giving welcome speeches during student intake week, at alumni garden parties, or faculty team-building events. Remember that it's the little things that often make a huge difference. For example, a dean could occasionally congratulate a student for having organized a successful event, or a professor for having published an exceptional paper that is highly relevant to the business community. While doing so is not always feasible, people are very aware of such gestures, as reports make their way around, generating goodwill and community belonging.

8.2   Lifelong Learning Liaisons, Not Study > Work > Retire

Over the next decade, advances in AI, robotics, and digitalization will significantly alter job requirements across various employment markets (Chui, Manyika, and Miremadi 2016). Such a shift will demand that workers acquire new competencies, skills, and knowledge throughout their professional lives; lifelong learning, reskilling, and upskilling have become undisputed parts of one's career (Ates and Alsal 2012; Bughin, Lund, and Hazan 2018; Kaplan 2021d). However, most business schools still focus on a linear, three-stage life model: you study, you work, and then you retire (Ishikura 2016). Not only is that model quickly going by the wayside, but in many management schools, the non-degree executive education division is separate from degree programs. In some cases, the former is even outsourced and disconnected from the degree-issuing institution. Instead, continuous education, as the term implies, should be a seamless continuum from undergraduate and graduate coursework. Lifelong learning provides an opportunity for creating long-term partnerships with students and alumni: yet another opportunity for community building.

Instead of a transactional model that considers students as one-time clients, a *relational model* should be employed toward forging lifelong learning liaisons with a business school's alumni. A relationship approach also fits better with the aforementioned nourishing mother meaning of alma mater (Dellarocas 2018). In a community of lifelong learners, students never really graduate; instead, the business school's mission is to continuously educate and nourish them, as a caring mentor would. In the future, teaching should be about providing adapted, long-term, customized content, which also works to build relationships, toward forming and cultivating a dynamic and loyal community (Ala et al. 2022).

To develop such lifelong relationships, and increase the chances of alumni thinking of their alma mater when the need to reskill arises, business schools should exploit the time when degree students are physically or digitally within their walls. It is during this period when educators and administrators can convince students of the importance of lifelong learning. Continuous learning offers could, for example, be communicated to students during a program's intake week, sending a strong message that learning is indeed a lifelong effort. Along the way, business schools should be bluntly transparent that an early-life degree will not suffice for one's entire professional career. Yet, looking at most institutions' marketing communications tells an entirely different story. Such "deceptive advertising" makes it harder to persuade current students, i.e., future alumni, that they'll still need formal education down the road.

Moreover, business schools should acquaint students with their continuous education divisions to show them their competencies therein. The school could, for example, offer students to audit selected executive education courses during their degree studies. Such experiences can prove that attending professional classes is a better option than watching YouTube tutorials for getting up to speed in a particular domain. Another strategy is to design courses in a way as to mix continuous education enrollees with early-life degree students. This could turn out to be a win-win situation, wherein executives are connected with potential new hires as they get a first-hand sense of what is important to soon-to-be graduates. Moreover, it is definitely an effective way of community building.

Yet another way to familiarize current students with continuous education is the introduction of a new kind of program structure that concludes with a period during which students already beginning their career are welcome to enroll in online courses and receive coaching. This will accustom students to the concept of lifelong learning, as well as constitute the beginning of a

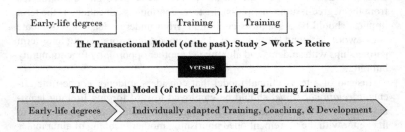

Figure 8.1 Lifelong Learning Liaisons vs. Study > Work > Retire

long-term, continuous relationship. Both Columbia and Harvard Business Schools are already introducing the notion of continuous education into their early-life programs: students are provided the possibility of extending certain degree programs over an extended period, enabling them to work part-time, better filling their current preferences and needs.

For a school's executive education offerings to appeal to alumni, and to divert them from enrolling in courses at competing institutions, business schools have several cards they can play. Most institutions already offer alumni significant discounts on continuing education. An even better idea may be introducing subscription models, similar to gym memberships, wherein continuous learners pay an annual fee in exchange for which they can enroll in a certain number of courses. Such a plan is already set for Northeastern University's (2016) academic plan for 2025. Hult Business School goes even further, offering alumni, free of charge, one elective course per year for life. While this might initially seem bad for Hult's bottom line, it's not only perfect in terms of long-term community management, but it could incentivize alumni taking advantage of this offer to enroll in additional, for-pay courses, or to give back to their alma mater in other ways.

Next to special offers for graduates, customization (Kaplan 2006; Mazurek and Malagocka 2022) of courses or course recommendations aimed at individual alumni act as a strong competitive advantage, persuading alumni to return to their alma mater continuously through their careers. To do so, business schools must invest in customer relationship management (CRM), which improves an institution's knowledge about individual alumni by accumulating individual information and preferences over time, thus enabling them to suggest the training best adapted to their profiles. Good CRM enables one's business school to be a perfect partner and coach in one's career path, helping alumni long beyond graduation (Johnson and Walker 2021).

Continuing education should also be offered to an institution's employees, for at least three reasons: firstly, both academic and non-academic staff need training to be on top of their game. Secondly, employees feel appreciated when their employer invests in them, thereby improving retention and reducing turnover – definitely good for community building. Thirdly is the matter of leading by example: how better to convince students and alumni of the importance of lifelong learning and the necessity of regularly returning to their alma mater than we, as educational providers, offer that to those in our employ?

Finally, business schools have an additional and unique card in their hands: we can make courses special in a way that only we can, for example, by combining modules with a class reunion wherein former classmates can learn together and reconnect. Learning in the same physical spaces as in the old days, or with an esteemed professor, can create powerful nostalgia. This is probably the best example of combining learning and teaching with forging a community around a business school, and of lifelong learning partnerships benefiting all concerned.

Last but not least: executive education and lifelong learning do not only serve the goal of community building, but also other goals as well: first of all, we want our alumni to be at the top of their games in their chosen careers, familiar with the latest academic insights in their domain. Secondly, it is also in our interest to connect between academics and business executives, potentially rendering faculty's research more relevant, as well as their teaching aligned with what businesses need. Thirdly, offering executive education can be highly profitable. Having said this, however, remember: an academically driven business school should not be about profit maximization, but rather about quality optimization. This applies to degree programs as well as executive education.

8.3   Buildings: Beyond Mere Brick-and-Mortar

Buildings go beyond brick-and-mortar (Kaplan 2021c); they're both literal and figurative cornerstones of community building (Temple 2008). We increasingly hear voices claiming that real estate for higher education is a thing of the past, and that courses will henceforth be taught online. This claim, however, dismisses the fact that university buildings fill functions besides instruction. Precisely because more and more courses take place online, buildings are more important than ever. While pre-Zoom classes, students and faculty commuted to campus to meet with each other, i.e., to teach and be taught, today that is less the case. Thus, cultivating community requires that buildings be welcoming and appealing enough to incentivize stakeholders to come to a campus (Muhammad, Sapri, and Sipan 2014) where "things are happening."

Real estate, therefore, must change to accommodate campus activities differently. There will be less need for lecture halls and dedicated classrooms, and more space dedicated to collaboration, teamwork, and simply inspiring conversations across the various stakeholder groups. If buildings create an appealing atmosphere, students, professors, alumni, and members of the surrounding community will come to campus and interact with each other, creating this vital attachment to and community spirit around their school. If a business school fails to attract stakeholders to campus, students and faculty in particular will instead "form a bond with" their home offices and laptops (Rovai and Wighting 2005).

While teaching won't be severed from physical buildings, what will be a thing of the past (or already should be) are top-down lectures in auditoriums. Such pedagogy is indeed better placed in the virtual sphere. What we will increasingly see is on-site teaching that is highly interactive, in adjustable, modular classrooms equipped with the latest technology. An example of such teaching is Yale's TEAL, or Technology-Enabled Active Learning classroom, which accommodates up to 100 students, seated at tables of 10 to 15 each, each with its own screen in addition to several additional screens placed around the room (Gould 2013). The professor gives short lectures lasting a few minutes, with each table discussing the material or working on a group assignment, thereby immediately putting into practice the just-heard theoretical explanations (Kaplan 2018).

Research collaborations and community building among academics from the same or differing disciplines can also be facilitated via physical plant structures and space adaptation. We already talked about why business schools should facilitate an inter- and multidisciplinary approach to teaching and learning. The same applies to research, and if properly designed, buildings can be a driving force to forge such collaboration across various disciplines. At the University of Texas, for example, researchers who want to work together on an interdisciplinary study can reserve space in a building adapted (or adaptable) to their needs. In enabling this, colleagues can physically meet for the time they need to advance their respective projects. When the project is over, professors return to their permanent offices or are assigned a new space for another interdisciplinary project. To ensure that such space is used mainly for inter- and multidisciplinary research projects, a review team comprised of faculty members evaluates each collaboration and is in charge of space allocation (Martinez 2020).

Ultimately, buildings are also important branding vectors, branding being an important driver for community building (Jeong 2021). A business school dedicated to sustainability should boast a sustainably operated campus that is energy efficient, contains ample recycling stations as well as circular economy elements, to mention just a few components of sustainability. A strongly international institution with multiple campuses across several countries could live-stream its various activities taking place in shared spaces on its campuses in order to visually convey activities in geographically dispersed locations being united and belonging to the same business school community. Finally, as mentioned earlier, the KLU brand is strengthened by the fact that its university building is located in one of the largest seaports in the world, which is known as Germany's "Gateway to the World" and is one of Hamburg's biggest attractions. The Kühne Logistics University campus thus offers an exceptional and much-appreciated view of the Elbe river, the port's busy container terminals, and the harbor's impressive cruise terminal, which accommodates, among others, the Queen Mary II.

I can't write about the importance of buildings without at least briefly addressing the online environment and virtual spaces of the future, where the metaverse especially will be an important online space. The idea of a highly immersive virtual world is not entirely new. Already when the virtual social world Second Life was in its heyday at the end of the 2000s, several universities and business schools such as INSEAD (Kaplan 2009) experimented with creating dedicated and branded spaces, in a few cases even holding virtual classes. However, the technology required for a high-quality, genuinely immersive experience was not yet there. In upcoming years, it will likely be a different story.

We must actively combine and coordinate online spaces with our school's physical spaces in order to create a no-borders environment enabling a seamless transition from one world to another. Remember: a community is about providing a platform for stakeholders to meet each other. The experience – whether online or live – should give a coherent picture and brand for community building to be most effective. To do so, an institution might replicate its physical buildings and floorplan in the metaverse, i.e., create "digital twins." The school could even stream real-time video from its physical buildings into the virtual environments and vice versa, i.e., screens throughout the physical campus onto which is projected what's happening on the metaverse campus.

When moving into the online sphere, we must take full advantage of the virtual opportunities. To illustrate, let's have a look at Nike's transition into the metaverse where, among other options, avatars can acquire virtual Nike sneakers, which are not only virtual copies of their physical counterparts, but feature integrated superpowers such as increased speed or the ability to jump an extralong distance. How does one acquire these superpowers? You must engage in some real-world exercise! To acquire the virtual superpowers, users must download an app, and according to the distance they walk in real life, their avatar's superpowers increase in the virtual sphere. Brilliant on Nike's part, utterly consistent with the brand's image: incentivizing physical exercise, during which Nike customers will wear their Nike gear, actively promoting the brand instead of sitting at their computers. Business schools are advised to develop such smart, brand-consistent, interlinkages between their physical and virtual spaces.

References

Ala M. Day I., Rasul T., Nair S., Baker M. (2022) Working adults' networking and social activities in lifelong learning. In A. Kaplan (ed.), *Digital transformation and disruption of higher education* (pp. 195–208). Cambridge University Press.

Andre E. K., Williams N., Schwartz F., Bullard C. (2017) Benefits of campus outdoor recreation programs: A review of the literature. *Journal of Outdoor Recreation, Education, and Leadership, 9*(1), 15–25.

Archbold J., O'Hagan J. (2011) *Student societies and clubs: Current structures and historical context, with special emphasis on arts/cultural societies.* Trinity Long Room Hub.

Ates H., Alsal K. (2012) The importance of lifelong learning has been increasing. *Procedia: Social and Behavioral Sciences, 46*, 4092–4096.

Balmer J. M. T., Liao M.-N., Wang W.-Y. (2010) Corporate brand identification and corporate brand management: How top business schools do it. *Journal of General Management, 35*(4), 77–102.

Bughin J., Lund S., Hazan E. (2018) Automation will make lifelong learning a necessary part of work. *Harvard Business Review*, May 24, available online at https://hbr.org/2018/05/automation-will-make-lifelong-learning-a-necessary-part-of-work.

Chui M., Manyika J., Miremadi M. (2016) Where machines could replace humans: And where they can't (yet). *McKinsey Quarterly*, July 8, 2016.

Dass S., Kabra S., Saxena V. N., Vinay M. (2020) Halo of trust: An integrative framework studying brand trust for business schools. *AIJR*, Abstracts, 33.

Dellarocas C. (2018) Higher education in a world where students never graduate, InsideHigherEd.com, August 1, 2018.

Gould S. (2013) Eight months later, TEAL classroom takes off. *Yale Daily News*, September 19, available online at: https://yaledailynews.com/blog/2013/09/19/eight-months-later-teal-classroom-takes-off/.

Ishikura Y. (2016) Study, work, retire: Time to scrap the old pattern of working life. World Economic Forum, October 27, available online at: https://www.weforum.org/agenda/2016/10/it-s-time-to-end-the-model-of-study-work-retire/.

Jeong C.-H. (2021) *"It looks like a proper business school now!": Legitimating buildings and building legitimacy*. University of Leicester.

Johnson J., Walker B. (2021) Digital transformation in university communications and marketing: Now is the time for university communicators to fully leap ahead into digital-first practices, as too much is at risk. *InsideHigherEd*, February 2, available online at: https://www.insidehighered.com/blogs/call-action-marketing-and-communications-higher-education/digital-transformation-university.

Kaplan A. (2006) *Factors influencing the adoption of mass customization: Determinants, moderating variables and cross-national generalizability*. Cuvillier.

Kaplan A. (2009) Virtual worlds and business schools: The case of INSEAD. In C. Wankel, J. Kingsley (eds.), *Higher education in virtual worlds: Teaching and learning in second life* (pp. 83–100). Emerald Group Publishing.

Kaplan A. (2018) A School is a Building that Has 4 Walls – with Tomorrow Inside": Toward the reinvention of the business school. *Business Horizons*, *61*(4), 599–608.

Kaplan A. (2021a) Branding and bonding: The key to competing in the Digital Age. EAIE – European Association for International Education, July 6, 2021, available online at https://www.eaie.org/blog/branding-bonding-competing-digital-age.html.

Kaplan A. (2021b) Higher education at the crossroads of disruption: The university of the 21st Century. In *Great debates in higher education*. Emerald Publishing.

Kaplan A. (2021c) More than just bricks and mortar. *LSE Higher Education Blog*, August 12, 2021, available online at https://blogs.lse.ac.uk/highereducation/2021/08/12/more-than-just-bricks-and-mortar/.

Kaplan A. (2021d) *Professionals need to keep their skills fresh. Will they turn to higher ed?* Harvard Business Publishing, September 17, 2021, available online at https://www.hbsp.harvard.edu/inspiring-minds/professionals-need-to-keep-their-skills-fresh-will-they-turn-to-higher-ed/?ab=top_nav.

Kaplan A. (2022) *Digital transformation and disruption of higher education*. Cambridge University Press.

Kaplan A., Haenlein M. (2009a) Consumer use and business potential of virtual worlds: The case of Second Life. *International Journal on Media Management*, *11*(3/4), 93–101.

Kaplan A., Haenlein M. (2009b) Consumers, companies, and virtual social worlds: A qualitative analysis of Second Life. *Advances in Consumer Research*, *36*(1), 873–874.

Kaplan A., Haenlein M. (2009c) The fairyland of Second Life: Virtual social worlds and how to use them. *Business Horizons*, *52*(6), 563–572.

Malagocka K., Mazurek G., Kaplan A. (2022) Virtual worlds, virtual reality, and augmented reality: Review, synthesis, and research agenda. In Z. Yan (ed.), *The Cambridge handbook of cyber behavior*. Cambridge University Press.

Martinez J. (2020) New building aims to promote interdisciplinary research. *UTEP Magazine*, January 22, 2020.

Mazurek G., Malagocka K. (2022) Personalisation of higher education: From prospects to alumni. In A. Kaplan (ed.), *Digital transformation and disruption of higher education* (pp. 289–300). Cambridge University Press.

McAlexander J. H., Schouten J. W., Koenig H. F. (2002) Building brand community. *Journal of Marketing*, 66(1), 38–54.

Muhammad S., Sapri M., Sipan I. (2014) Academic buildings and their influence on students' wellbeing in higher education institutions. *Social Indicators Research*, 115, 1159–1178.

Muniz A. A., O'Guinn T. C. (2001) Brand community. *Journal of Consumer Research*, 27(4), 412–432.

Northeastern University (2016) *Academic Plan: Northeastern 2025*, Northeastern University, retrieved August 26, 2020, https://www.northeastern.edu/academic -plan/plan/.

Petriglieri G., Petriglieri J. (2010) Identity workspaces: The case of business schools. *Academy of Management Learning and Education*, 9(1), 44–60.

Rovai A. P., Wighting M. J. (2005) Feelings of alienation and community among higher education students in a virtual classroom. *The Internet and Higher Education*, 8(2), 97–110.

Temple P. (2008) Learning spaces in higher education: An under-researched topic. *London Review of Education*, 6(3), 229–241.

9 Top Leadership's Trouble in Taking the Lead

By now, it should be clear that there's lots to do in this digital and virtual era that business schools worldwide face (cf. Chapters 1 and 2). The sector's digital disruption is likely right around the corner, with how business schools currently function possibly rendered redundant (cf. Chapter 3; Kaplan 2021a, 2022; Kaplan and Haenlein 2016). Management and business research needs to be rethought, reimagined, and considered a compelling element for an institution's positioning and branding (cf. Chapters 4 and 7). Teaching must be more and more viewed as one component in a larger package providing students with a wholistic and integrated experience, including individualized coaching, internships, study trips, and extracurriculars (cf. Chapter 5). Lifelong learning relationships will need to be cultivated and developed, replacing the current study > work > retire formula (Kaplan 2021c; cf. Chapter 8). Last but not least, business schools are expected to take strong stances on societal issues such as climate change, inequality, and migration and displacement.

To survive and thrive in this post-pandemic landscape, business schools must strongly differentiate themselves from each other, as well as from the new edtech and big tech entrants (cf. Chapter 7). Intensive community building is the way to stay on top of the game (cf. Chapter 8). Help can be found from accreditation bodies and rankings if and only if these are employed to improve, not to impress (cf. Chapter 6). All this demands swift and resolute change management. A clear vision and operative plan must be drafted. Implementation will require willingness to make tough decisions backed by strong persuasive skills from business schools' leadership teams. In brief, business schools will need experienced academics with solid management and leadership skills at the top of their organizational pyramids, willing and able to take the lead on their institution's path in this challenging but exciting journey (Schlegelmilch 2020).

Especially in unstable times, an academic institution is dependent on its dean, president, rector, vice-chancellor, or whatever the top administrators' titles might be, to guide the community's stakeholders successfully into the future. To do so, a dean must be a dreamer who designs a compelling vision. S/he also needs to be a doer capable of implementing it, and a darer courageous enough to make certain tough and likely unpopular decisions, navigating the

DOI: 10.4324/9781003343509-9

ship through the (mostly digital) storm on the horizon. Moreover, a dean should be a respected scholar (as s/he represents an academic institution), an experienced manager (often in charge of hundreds of academic and non-academic employees), and a leader (defining and leading the way and path to come). A business school dean is a jack-of-all-trades and master of one (i.e., in most cases one academic discipline), bringing together the worlds of academia and management. Captain Jack's leadership style and technique are not to be dismissed: higher education has a peculiar, negatively inclined relationship to power, often avoiding it as much as possible. Therefore, instead of an emperor at the top of the business school, a dean needs to be a nurturer, motivator, and especially empowerer.

9.1   Vision and Venture

Every organization needs a coherent idea and clear roadmap. Especially in turbulent times, vision is vital. Management schools and higher education in general are at the crossroads of potential disruption (Kaplan 2021a). They thus need to come up with a new and differentiating vision, decisive for their destiny. Business school deans must be visionaries, capable of designing a strong vision, similar to the founders of the first management schools (Kaplan 2014; Thomas and Cornuel 2012). ESCP's establishment, for example, followed the avant-garde vision and inspiration of French businessman Vital Roux to teach a new profession – the manager – and to establish a school where pedagogy would be based on simulated business operations, which over time increase in complexity (Nioche 1997). Joseph Wharton, American industrialist and founder of the first US business school, also had a clear and unwavering vision of a school focused on training the future leaders of society's public and private sectors. Wharton stated during the Second Industrial Revolution that the Wharton School should "instill a sense of the coming strife" in commercial activity (Wharton 1880). Similarly, when the German entrepreneur Klaus-Michael Kühne decided to found KLU, his vision was clear: to build the world's leading university for logistics, supply chain, and transport to increase and promote the attractiveness of supply chain and operations management as an academic subject and research field.

Creating a vision in higher education, however, is not an easy endeavor. On the one hand, you're limited by legal constraints and compliance with national and international academic requirements. On the other hand, you want to launch the entire community on the journey inspired by your vision. For your vision and its implementation to be effective, you need significant buy-in from your school's various stakeholder groups, who may or may not agree with you, or with each other (Olivier, Brown, and Lewis 2014). Alumni might be hesitant about change due to nostalgia for their student days. Current students might be worried that your vision will reduce their chances of getting a good job upon graduation, and that they're enrolled in an institution that differs from "what they signed up for." Faculty might oppose what they fear will be an increase in their workload or a change in the nature of their professional activities. It's therefore the dean's job to unite the institution's stakeholders behind a clear and unified vision, and motivate them to collaborate in a dynamic community of academic and non-academic staff, students and alumni, and the various external stakeholders. The priorities and preoccupations of these various groups must be balanced and coordinated, with the dean at the control panels.

This is all the more important, as a vision not only needs to be designed, but thereafter implemented. The more a business school's community supports the vision, the easier its implementation will be. In addition to a dean being visionary, s/he also must be keen on taking action and transforming a vision into a real venture. S/he must be a doer, or in the words of Neumann and Neumann (1999): deans who successfully transform their institutions and prepare them for the digital transformation and new competitive landscape will exhibit strong leadership qualities with an innovative vision, strategic focus, and an entrepreneurial mindset. As venture-oriented, rapid-output, for-profit educational start-ups and big tech giants enter the management education sector, business school deans must be able to turn a vision into concrete steps and measures, show high reactivity, – or even better, proactivity – and pivot to adapt to market changes.

Business schools face a period of instability and intense transformation. Successful implementation of an institution's vision will demand some heavy-duty change management (Bass 1985): deans will need to dare to radically alter autochthonous structures, possibly rendering their venture an adventure. Throughout the pandemic, it became evident that change management is an essential skill to have as a dean, critical when s/he is expected to navigate an institution over exceptionally uncertain terrain. A dean incapable of managing change, will him- or herself be managed by it. Agility needs to replace bureaucracy (Pucciarelli and Kaplan 2016, 2019).

However, making clear and tough decisions does not mean that a business school should adopt a pure business-like modus operandi. Deans are confronted with the difficult task of finding an equilibrium between ensuring high-quality academia and complying with increasingly business- and market-driven reasoning (Pucciarelli and Kaplan 2016). This balancing act translates, inter alia, into treating students like customers in all non-academic matters, while considering them to be stakeholders in everything related to pedagogy and learning. This means that a solid service orientation should be applied in such activities as helping students with visa applications or searching for housing. Course and curricula design, however, stays within the purview of faculty. It becomes essential for business schools to be (even more) viewed as rigorous academic institutions, so as to differentiate themselves from profit-oriented alternatives entering the market. In a future of inexpensive study options offered by ed and big tech, the stereotype of "buying" one's diploma will become detrimental to the academic sector.

One indication of the increasing awareness of the need for change in management and business schools is institutions having added "executive" to the titles of their top administration, i.e., the dean has become the "executive dean" and the president the "executive president," based on the Latin origin of "executive" meaning "getting things done." Yet, changing a title doesn't change its holder's skill set. Future deans will need to be visionary entrepreneurs (Pucciarelli and Kaplan 2016), to a certain extent explorers, who accept the possibility of the sector's disruption in this post-pandemic era. Given what is at stake and considering the task's growing complexity, the deanship and business school presidency increasingly have shifted from roles that previously were internally elected, mostly by faculty members and colleagues, to positions that are in more and more cases externally filled with the help of executive headhunters (Davies 2014).

9.2   Academia and Management

It should by now be apparent that in a period driven by intensive change, deans must exhibit strong management skills, so that one could legitimately ask whether an academic is the best person for the job. While it is true that management requires experience, a dean should first and foremost be a scholar, for several reasons: firstly, an academic institution not being led by an academic is inconsistent and illogical; as the top administrator of a business school, a dean represents it to the outside; not being an academic would complicate this task. Remember that being considered an academic institution is one of the differentiating elements to new, less academic market entrants. A dean's legitimacy vis-à-vis faculty would likewise suffer if s/he did not have a strong academic background (Davies 2016). To lead a group of professors, who tend to have firm beliefs and opinions, a dean needs to understand what it takes to conduct relevant and responsible research (Haenlein et al. 2022), to prepare a good class session and deliver high-quality pedagogy, and finally, to comprehend and thoroughly value the principle of academic freedom.

Consequently, a deanship is a management position bringing together the points of view of both the academic and managerial worlds (Currie 2014). As dean, you not only represent your institution and lead the business school faculty. You manage the support staff, are in charge of budgets, buildings, branding, and a variety of other domains. For most of us – especially us academics – management skills are not inborn, and thus must be learned. These are acquired on the job and in the best case, their complexity increases gradually, not abruptly. Over my career, I've seen academics (including myself) reaching leadership positions and overnight being in charge of 20, 50, 500, or more employees without having any previous management experience.

Most of them were initially overwhelmed thereby (Davies 2015). Knowing and teaching management theories does not translate into being equipped to immediately manage a team. In my experience having headed ESCP Business

School's Branding, Communications, and Marketing Division, I can affirm that while certainly useful, my knowledge as a marketing and communications professor was not nearly sufficient to effectively master and manage this division. Managing non-academics also differs vastly from managing academics, let alone a team of PhD students. Actually, you do not manage professors, you coordinate them. In brief, in academia, it is not uncommon for academics to get propelled into leadership positions without any prior management experience, and the result is in more than a few cases, not a good one.

To be fair, scholars rarely plan their careers with the explicit aim of one day serving in an administration position (Currie 2014, Davis 2015). They usually become academics because they want to conduct research or because they love teaching, or both. In most cases, taking on management responsibility is not on their agenda, and rather happens through a combination of circumstances. Academia and management are in many ways opposites. Thus an academic entering a management position not only must learn how management functions; s/he must *un*learn several elements of being a scholar.

Firstly, academics are not trained in rapid decision-making, in particular, if such decisions must be made under high uncertainty and likely will not make everybody happy. Academics are groomed within their academic disciplines, and operate in a very collegiate context. They're used to discussing academic matters and differing viewpoints without necessarily feeling the urge to reach one solution to a problem. Differing opinions is accepted in the academic world. Data confirms (or not) a hypothesis developed under certain assumptions. Moreover, publishing one's research can take years, so that professors are used to things taking time. A dean, in contrast, is expected to reach decisions quickly, and often with little data or information at hand. Consequently, inexperienced deans either try to maintain the status quo, to postpone decisions until more information is available (which in most cases never happens), or to find some compromise aimed at making everybody happy, which ultimately often has the opposite effect. Instead of academic rigor and patience, agility and guts are a dean's job requirements.

Secondly, academic rigor not only complexifies decision-making, but also acts as a barrier to a dean's ability to delegate. Research and teaching demand attention to detail and precision. Scholars are used to meticulously drafting and reworking hypotheses, applying highly advanced methodologies, and so forth. In addition, they usually work on their own: they prepare and teach their courses; they work autonomously on their research or in very small teams, with everybody aware of all elements of the project. In short, professors are used to being in charge and in control of every aspect of their work. To delegate and give up such control does not come naturally to them, and often turns into micromanaging, with professors by definition accustomed to correcting and coaching. A dean, on the other hand, usually is in charge of hundreds of people, rendering delegating essential to the smooth running of the business school.

Thirdly, an academic remains an academic even when serving as a dean, making it extremely stressful for them to make decisions and/or reforms that could be perceived negatively by their peers and previous (and hopefully future) colleagues. Many if not most deans will at some point reintegrate into the school as a professor, and go back to their roots, so to speak (Bradshaw 2015); at least the option is in the back of every dean's mind. This can in many cases result in unconsciously unbalanced decisions, whereas good community building requires precisely the opposite, i.e., equal treatment of all stakeholder groups. This tendency is exacerbated by the fact that deans who are familiar with academia, in many cases feel obligated to explain to their Boards of Directors how professors function, which can prompt them to take on the struggle for extra budgets and better work conditions for their colleagues, instead of pushing changes and strategic decisions downwards for the good of the entire institution.

It is precisely in these situations when a manager goes beyond mere management, and becomes a leader. Or, in the words of Peter Drucker (1963, 1974) efficiency means doing things right, while effectiveness means doing the right things. Translated into "deanspeak," Drucker's words might be paraphrased to "While management is doing things right, leadership is doing the right things." A successful dean must be a leader, with his or her leadership skills developing and being honed over time. Yet, business schools are surprisingly inactive in developing leadership qualities in their ranks (Kaplan 2021c), which would mean providing so-called high-potentials with targeted leadership training and continuing education to improve their management competences (Davies 2013). While this might seem ironic, it makes sense, as it can feel embarrassing to need training in areas that you yourself teach. After all, how can a professor in a management discipline need to learn management? This might be where an academic needs to go above and beyond her innate competencies in order to become a qualified manager and experienced leader.

9.3   (Em)power and Motivate

In order to effectively lead, any leader needs a certain degree of power (Pfeffer 2010). However, "I do not have any power" is recurringly heard from top administrators in the higher education sector (Blackmore and Sachs 2012). They assert that their actions are hampered by government regulations, those in the organization to whom they report, and opposition of those over whom they officially do have power, i.e., mainly faculty (Lumby 2019). While this is true to a certain extent (MacIntosh, Jack, and O'Gorman 2014), such a mindset can lead to self-fulfilling prophecy, with business school deans rendered powerless, at least when considering one of the defining characteristics of power, i.e., the ability to act or produce an effect. Consequently, an institution might find itself with someone in a position of power feeling powerless, uncomfortable with making decisions, or scared to take resolute actions. They may even hide their lack of management and leadership skills behind this claim of not having any power. Being thus paralyzed might not be a problem when things run smoothly. But in times of substantial transformations, deans are compelled to make decisions, which if made by someone not equipped to do so, might appear incomprehensible and/or erratic.

What is certain is that academics – not to mention most people – do not like to be told what to do in a coercive manner. "It's easier to move a cemetery than a faculty" is a well-known saying in higher education (Rousseau 2012). Academic freedom, essentially academia's principle that nobody can tell you what to teach or focus your research on, provides professors, rightly so, complete freedom in these matters. Scholars are not used to hierarchy in their core activities, and in some cases transfer this feeling beyond these areas. Especially in settings wherein the dean is elected exclusively by her faculty colleagues, this might lead to suboptimal outcomes. When choosing their future leader, faculty not infrequently apply criteria with which they are familiar: the candidate's research and teaching quality. Previous management experience or leadership skills do not always play an important role. It even happens that the faculty elects the candidate who is least likely to make bold decisions or complex changes, so as to maintain what they perceive to be *their* power. To a degree, this is even understandable when choosing between an inactive bad or inexperienced manager and an equally bad one who is eager to make a lot of changes or has her own agenda (Bryman 2007).

While I've painted a simplified picture of what goes on in higher education, and circumstances vary between national systems and institutional contexts (Davies 2015), it can certainly be said that power in academia is perceived somewhat negatively (Peck 2011). This, however, is viewing the glass as half empty. Alongside coercion, control, and dominance, the term "power" also implies nurturance, inspiration, and trust building. Applying the latter is how leadership in higher education can be highly effective and, indeed, powerful. Most academics – indeed, most people – have no problem with this version of power. We feel cooperative when we understand decisions, are made aware of the situation and context, and feel being listened to. Power in higher education works by relationship building, motivation, and empowerment.

The building of relationships is certainly one way of being able to exert power. People need to feel that they can trust their leadership team, and if they do, they are likely to support its decisions. Trust is built over time, i.e., when the various stakeholder groups learn that they can count on their leaders' words and promises. Nothing is worse for building trust than telling people what they want to hear and then turning around and doing whatever it is you planned. The same applies to leadership not following its own rules. Leading by example is essential. Preaching the importance of sustainability, for example, but leading an unsustainable lifestyle oneself, will cause one to lose credibility (Kaplan 2021b). This does not mean being perfect, but rather being authentic. To continue the sustainability example, a leader

admitting hesitations with certain aspects of sustainable living, while applying sustainability in other domains, is acceptable: as opposed to hypocrisy,
admitting vulnerability creates trustworthy relationships, again leading to
power.

Motivating and inspiring teams can be equally powerful. As Lorange
(2000) puts it, leaders manage to implement their vision and balance various stakeholders through inspiration, motivation, and charisma. On the
other hand, people need to understand where a leader wants the institution
to evolve, and what is important to them. Stakeholders need to be aligned on
an organization's direction and priorities. They need clarity and transparency.
Charismatic and inspirational deans are able to convince their stakeholders
why a particular action or decision benefits the institution, and in turn, its
stakeholders. Steady internal communication is of the essence. In my experience, even if you believe that you don't have anything to internally communicate at a given time, holding regular staff meetings is recommended: while
you may not feel a need to talk, your employees might very much feel a need
to.

Empowering others renders a leader more powerful (Dambe and Moorad
2008). Giving an individual power can link that individual to the power-giver,
as without the giver's power, the individual will not continue to benefit from
the authority bestowed upon her. Moreover, creating infrastructures and processes that enable others to do their work properly increases a leader's esteem.
Instead of an emperor, a business school needs an empowerer, not only for
staff and faculty, but also for students who want to improve their experience,
or alumni who want to give back to their alma mater. Thus empowering your
various stakeholder groups not only strengthens the sense of community, but
enables the dean to make powerful decisions and actions.

I can confirm from my own experience that a higher education institution
can only be successfully led via inspiration, motivation, trust, transparency,
and empowerment of others. Leadership asks for power – in the positive
sense; coercion, control, and dominance are counterproductive. The same
applies to hiding behind claims of lack of authority and subsequent inac-
tion. When you hear an academic administrator say that s/he does not have
any power, it most likely indicates a complete misunderstanding of the role,
weak leadership and management skills, or just laziness. Leadership without
power is impossible, and strong leaders see the glass of power within higher
education as half full.

In reality, leaders as depicted in Figure 9.1 are rare, and the experience
and skill set demanded by the task are hard to find (Kaplan 2018). It feels
like the position of dean needs to be filled by a jack-of-all-trades: s/he needs
to be a dreamer, a doer, and a darer. In terms of powerful, s/he must engage
in nurturing, motivation, and empowerment. And of course the ideal dean
should be an experienced and trained manager and leader. Additionally,
in order to credibly represent a business school internally and especially

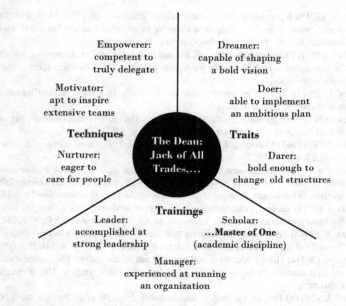

Figure 9.1 The Dean: Jack of All Trades, Master Of One

externally, the jack-of-all-trades needs to be a respected scholar in at least one academic field. It is obviously impossible to find a profile that ticks all these boxes, and most likely many more. Ultimately, it's a question of where to put the cursor and what competences are needed most in a given period and context. In times of little change necessary, a world-acclaimed academic is certainly the perfect choice to helm an institution. In times of groundbreaking reforms to implement, a more managerially competent and experienced, yet less renowned academic, might be the wiser pick (Kring and Kaplan 2011).

References

Bass B. M. (1985) *Leadership and performance beyond expectations*. Free Press.

Blackmore J., Sachs, J. (2012) *Performing and reforming leaders: Gender, educational restructuring, and organizational change*. SUNY Press.

Bradshaw D. (2015) *Short tenure of deans signals a leadership void*. ft.com, April 27.

Bryman A. (2007) *Effective leadership in higher education: Summary of findings*. Leadership Foundation.

Currie G. (2014) Hybrid managers in business schools. In *Building the leadership capacity of UK business schools* (pp. 12–13). Association of Business Schools.

Dambe M., Moorad F. (2008) From power to empowerment: A paradigm shift in leadership. *South African Journal of Higher Education, 22*(3), 575–587.

Davies J. (2013) Revitalising the business school leadership pipeline: How will we source future deans? In *ABS, Is it Possible to Balance Student Demands with Business Needs?* (pp. 81–94). Association of Business Schools.

Davies J. (2014) Future-proofing the UK business school deanship: Chartering horses for new courses. In *Building the leadership capacity of UK business schools* (pp. 7–9). Association of Business Schools.

Davies J. (2015) *Reflections on the role of the business school dean.* Chartered Association of Business Schools.

Davies J. (2016) Are business school deans doomed? The global financial crisis, Brexit and all that. *Journal of Management Development, 35*(7), 901–915.

Drucker P. F. (1963) Managing for business effectiveness. *Harvard Business Review, 41*(3), 53–60.

Drucker P. F. (1974) *Management. tasks, responsibilities, practices.* London: Heinemann.

Haenlein M., Bitner M. J., Kohli A. K., Lemon K. N., Reibstein D. J. (2022) Responsible research in marketing. *Journal of the Academy of Marketing Science, 50*(1), 8–12.

Kaplan A. (2014) European management and European business schools: Insights from the history of business schools. *European Management Journal, 32*(4), 529–534.

Kaplan A. (2018) "A school is a building that has 4 walls – with tomorrow inside": Toward the reinvention of the business school. *Business Horizons, 61*(4), 599–608.

Kaplan A. (2021a) Higher education at the crossroads of disruption: The university of the 21st century. In *Great debates in higher education.* Bingley, UK: Emerald Publishing.

Kaplan A. (2021b) Prepare for student sustainability demands to go through the roof. *Times Higher Education,* October 19, available online at https://www.timeshigher education.com/campus/prepare-student-sustainability-demands-go-through-roof.

Kaplan A. (2021c) *Professionals need to keep their skills fresh. Will they turn to higher ed?* Harvard Business Publishing, September 17, 2021, available online at https://www.hbsp.harvard.edu/inspiring-minds/professionals-need-to-keep-their-skills-fresh-will-they-turn-to-higher-ed/?ab=top_nav.

Kaplan A. (2022) *Digital transformation and disruption of higher education.* Cambridge: Cambridge University Press.

Kaplan A., Haenlein M. (2016) Higher education and the digital revolution: About MOOCs, SPOCs, Social Media, and the Cookie Monster. *Business Horizons, 59*(4), 441–450.

Kring K., Kaplan S. (2011) *The business school dean redefined: New leadership requirements from the front lines of change in academia.* Los Angeles: Korn/Ferry Institute.

Lorange P. (2000) Setting strategic direction in academic institutions: The case of the business school. *Higher Education Policy, 13*(4), 399–413.

Lumby J. (2019) Leadership and power in higher education. *Studies in Higher Education, 44*(9), 1619–1629.

MacIntosh R., Jack G., O'Gorman K. (2014) Who'd be a dean? Leadership in a low-authority environment. In *Building the leadership capacity of UK business schools* (pp. 18–20). London: Association of Business Schools.

Neumann Y., Neumann E. F. (1999) The president and the college bottom line: The role of strategic leadership styles. *International Journal of Educational Management, 13*(2), 73–81.

Nioche J. P. (1997) Pratique et théorie dans l'enseignement de la gestion: Une perspective historique, Intervention à l'école de Paris du management, May 20,

available online: https://www.google.com/url?sa=t&rct=j&q=&esrc=s&source
=web&cd=&ved=2ahUKEwik8fClhP34AhVQXfEDHaVYCdUQFnoECAMQ
AQ&url=https%3A%2F%2Fecole.org%2Ffr%2Fdownload-seance-cr%2F165
&usg=AOvVaw0REd1lwgQiLbjRJ7piNB38.

Olivier N., Brown A., Lewis M. (2014) Business school deans: Leadership in a complex, multi-stakeholder environment. In *Building the leadership capacity of UK business schools* (pp. 21–24). London: Association of Business Schools.

Peck E. (2011) Hierarchy in universities: What it is with leadership, power and authority? *The Guardian*, December 1.

Pfeffer J. (2010) Power play. *Harvard Business Review*, July–August, 84–92.

Pucciarelli F., Kaplan A. (2016) Competition and strategy in higher education: Managing complexity and uncertainty. *Business Horizons, 59*(3), 311–320.

Pucciarelli F., Kaplan A. (2019) Competition in higher education. In B. Nguyen, T. C. Melewar, J. Hemsley-Brown (eds.) *Strategic brand management in higher education.* New York: Routledge.

Rousseau D. M. (2012) Designing a better business school: Channelling Herbert Simon, addressing the critics, and developing actionable knowledge for professionalizing managers. *Journal of Management Studies, 49*(3), 600–618.

Schlegelmilch B. (2020) Why business schools need radical innovations: Drivers and development trajectories. *Journal of Marketing Education, 42*(2), 93–107.

Thomas H., Cornuel E. (2012) Business schools in transition? Issues of impact, legitimacy, capabilities, and re-invention. *Journal of Management Development, 31*(4), 329–335.

Wharton J. (1880) Letter to Friends, December 6, available online at https://alumni.wharton.upenn.edu/wharton-fund/letter-joseph-wharton/.

Afterword
It's [about] the Student, Stupid!

Remember the declaration, "It's the economy, stupid?" Coined by campaign strategist James Carville during Bill Clinton's 1992 US presidential run, this phrase was internally directed at the campaign's team to remind them that any plans, actions, or talking points should focus on the economy, which at the time was in a recession. Internalizing this phrase and strategy won Clinton the presidency, unseating the incumbent George H.W. Bush. Applying this logic to the future success of business schools, top leadership teams are advised to internalize that "It's about the student!"

Throughout this book, I explained and analyzed in several instances the importance of student-centricity in managing education's digital transformation and potential disruption. To some extent, history is repeating itself with business schools returning to their origins, when their focus was on pedagogy and student training, and their development into educated, skilled leaders. Except that now, new entrants from the ed and big tech sectors provide less costly and briefer alternatives to business school programs with their ever-rising tuition. In several cases, these up-and-coming and innovative players not only lead their graduates to job market success, but they also deliver more up-to-date content due to more flexibility and less regulatory constraints; and hire high-profile (or "celeb") practitioners as their instructors. Business schools will need to compete in this new landscape and prove that their longer and more costly programs result in better qualified and more competent managers and entrepreneurs than do graduates of Google's Career Certificates or LinkedIn Learning, for example.

Business schools will also face fiercer competition between each other, with previously distant institutions having gotten very close to prospective students, in digital terms. Moreover, the sector's digitalization leads to far more transparency in at least two domains: firstly, potential enrollees increasingly can experience an institution's pedagogical quality by participating in MOOCs, watching YouTube videos of professors' classes, or by simply watching a current student's recordings of a couple of their online courses. Secondly, candidates can easily find out where a given program's graduates end up employment-wise without having to trust the institution's brochure or website, as a simple LinkedIn search will do the trick. In fact, LinkedIn could

DOI: 10.4324/9781003343509-10

just as easily create their own business school ranking by analyzing users' job profiles and alma maters. This could be a game-changer for established, longstanding league tables that up until now vouched for business schools' quality.

Ultimately, it comes down to making a business program worth students' while. Current business school tuition might not be too high if students feel that they really get value for their (or their parents') money, i.e., they ordinarily complain only if they have the opposite impression. A simple way of becoming more student-centric would be to ask them what they actually expect from studying at a business school, or more precisely, at your school. When was the last time you organized focus groups with your students? What do your students consider as high value and what not? What do you need to add to your programs and what could you stop doing without reducing value in your students' eyes? Long program durations can be justified by providing a completely integrated, coordinated, and value-adding experience across academic courses, internships, study abroad, extracurriculars, and a top-notch career service helping graduates to find their dream job. And by "dream job," I don't necessarily mean the job that pays the most, but rather the one that the graduate finds most fulfilling. Business schools must become platforms integrating these areas in such a way as to efficiently and effectively cultivate the student to become a highly trained, competent manager and leader.

Thus any component of a business school should authentically and genuinely promote its students' future employability and success in their careers (and why not general life happiness as well?). Allow me to (re)give you some examples:

Providing an active research environment might lead to attracting better professors, i.e., the best pedagogues and teachers, which would benefit students. However, the recruiting of pure researchers who are not strong in pedagogy, does not align with student-centricity. When putting courses online, the question must be what is most efficacious in terms of pedagogy and student development, and not what might be the cheapest and logistically most efficient option. Therefore, budgets should be allocated in such a way as to optimize student-centricity: in some cases, as aforementioned, budget considerations could justify putting courses online, then allocating the resources freed up thereby to potentially higher-value activities such as the student and alumni career services and support. Such a move, however, must remain the exception, and should only be implemented if academic quality does not suffer. After all, a business school is first and foremost an academic institution, and in the future must be considered as such even more so.

Given this argument's importance, student-centricity does not mean making decisions in a way that leaves other stakeholders dissatisfied. The contrary should be the case: if faculty and administrative staff do not feel appreciated, they won't give their best to students. In the long run, business school leadership needs to make everybody happy by building a dynamic community

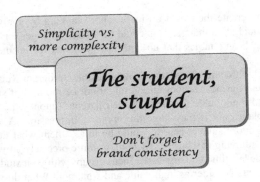

Figure 10.1 Afterword: It's [about] the Student, Stupid!

consisting of all internal and external stakeholders – yet, ultimately prioritizing the students. Nor does this mean not challenging students academically. Again, the opposite is the case: academic requirements should be high to ensure that students are optimally prepared for their future jobs. I said it before and I'll say it again: business schools need to stress their being academic institutions to differentiate themselves from the alternative educational providers.

In my experiences serving in various business school leadership positions, I've come to the conclusion that while this sector is definitely highly complex, undoubtedly complicated, wildly entangled, firmly constrained, and strongly regulated, this renders decision-making all the more simple: we just need to ask ourselves three questions when facing a difficult decision:

1. How will the students benefit from a given decision? What will lead to improving their employability and chances of having a fulfilling career while leading a joyful life? Again, this does not mean worsening the conditions of the other stakeholders. But ultimately, it definitely is about the students.
2. Is the decision coherent with the institution's brand? I extensively explained the advantages, and necessity in the digital era, of a strong brand such as visibility in the job market and the importance of brand consistency to get there. Often decisions become quite easy when applying the branding question, given that you know what your business school stands for.
3. Will the decision increase or decrease organizational complexity? In the long run, aiming for simplicity is better for any institution, and as such, for business students. The schools with which I'm familiar rarely capitalize on what they already have and do. Rather they continuously add new projects and activities, i.e., complexity. This, however, doesn't mean that you cannot develop new, better (brand-fitting) activities if these replace old structures, habits, or ventures.

Obviously, those readers who have served in leadership positions know that there are occasionally situations where you need to make decisions that don't align with these guidelines for political or economic reasons, especially when it's a question of survival. Nonetheless, I've seen only a few instances wherein deviating from these principles is justified. In particular regarding politics, in cases where university leadership is compelled to play the political game far too often, they might consider moving on, as the preoccupation with politics can in fact reduce a business school dean's value significantly, with possible negative consequences for the institution.

But this is me: you need to adapt to your situation and interpret what you've read here according to your institution, management, and leadership style. This was my intention: to provide advice, inspiration, food for thought, vision, perspective, and outlook. I immensely enjoyed writing this book; and hope you enjoyed reading it. Business schools and higher education in general is an exciting, largely gratifying, and dynamic sector in which to work. Most likely, dynamics will increase, as will excitement. Over the last two centuries, business schools have showed resilience. I believe – actually, I'm convinced – that they will do so going forward.

Index

**Page numbers in bold reference tables.
**Page numbers in italics reference figures.

Printed in the United States
by Baker & Taylor Publisher Services